The Teachings of Don Luan:

A Rocky Way of Knowledge

Bastion St. James

Ember Press

for my wife

Aaron

subdivisions

The Teachings of Don Luan

preface

This is a true story.

My new friend Donald Luan gazed at me with a look I had rarely seen before. This man held an air of wisdom so uncommon in mankind that for many such can seem extraterrestrial.

'There was once a boy, Bastion,' he began as he handed me a cold glass of iced limeade. Then he sat in what I thought might be his favorite chair—overstuffed—and motioned me to one equally as comfortable, 'This boy was raised by people who, for whatever reason, refused to let him be the person he was made to be. He was taught that he had to fit into some mold or another, but this made him angry and confused, because the world had never made much sense to him to begin with. So, because of his confusion, he even began treating others younger than himself in the very same way that he was being treated—callously. He became filled with the poisons of hopelessness and remorse and hatred for those who mistreated him. He had no interest in understanding them, in understanding the plight of humanity—even in really understanding himself. Fame is what he thought he wanted. He believed strongly in freedom of expression and in being the person he had been created to be, yet his wounds made him afraid and often violent, his fear making him develop boundaries for himself and for others. One day he realized that this was what had also happened to those who had hurt him, and he began to pray for their souls, and was able one day to readily forgave them all—from his heart. Time went on, and as he grew older and stronger of mind and limb, he gave that selfsame heart to his King—the Peer of the Realm. Over time, he grew to love his Liege-Lord more than he loved his own soul, and would do anything for his King. This loyalty he declared openly so often that soon enough he caught the attention of the King himself, and was therefore summoned to visit the inner court of the palace. When the young warrior presented himself before the Peer, he was immediately put to martial test by quick and brutal knights of the court—the King's own private guard. True enough, the King saw that this battler had not merely declared his love in order to receive the praise of other men, but would, and could, fight to the death if necessary for the realm and the name of its ruler. Overcoming every attack tactic used by the brutal guard, this loving warrior was that very day made the king's champion, and handed the task of retraining the elite guards of the court who had lost to his hand. So, time went on, and the yearly round of battles came, it being the springtime, when kings go out to war. Wishing to secure his borders which had been encroached upon by the armies of foreign rulers, the Peer of the Realm called for his new champion to not only fight alongside him in conflict, but to serve as a battle-breaker, a *berserker*, one who would lead other warriors with his ferocity and fearlessness. Because of the great sins of the people, however, that season of battle proved to be a terribly bloody one, yet, nevertheless, a victorious one for the King and his armies. The King's champion, though, the most feared warrior on the battlefield in anybody's memory, grew, through many atrocious fights, a battle-weary soul, and so, one day in an inexplicable fit of madness, he left his Liege's side in search of rest and oasis. It greatly saddened the King that his champion did not come home to the palace for the needed reprieve he sought, but rather chose to become a wandering vagabond, a mendicant dressed in rags who carried nothing but an empty bowl and a water bag. Throughout his travels on land and sea, he maintained his presence as a warrior, but when he was challenged by younger fighters, he would only smile, turn his head away, and keep moving. Seeing that he offered no resistance, the youthful challengers would leave him be. Others, however, avoided him—those who knew him and remembered his violent prowess on the battlefield, his unyielding ability to cut great swaths through tried and true enemy warriors as a reaper cuts swaths with his scythe through a field of ripened wheat or rye. His eyes held an inner fire that, alas, would not die—an insatiable hunger for a renewed and fervent love of his Liege-Lord and the inner court where he had known his greatest joy. As it happened, after many years of wondering and waiting, the King finally called for his horse and himself set out to search for his dearly loved champion—for he had sent many messengers in the past to look for his friend, and all had come back to court without him, their hands thrown high in frustration. Some brought word that the warrior had involved himself in this or that enterprise, or had fallen beneath this spell or another, but none were able to coerce him to come back to the sanctuary of the palace. Yet this world-weary battler would not, after all, escape his Lord, for how can a king be a faithful and righteous ruler if he can be conquered by his own champion? So, the Peer of the Realm searched for a number of years until one day he spied his warrior friend sitting with a beautiful girl by a placid bay. The King knew from a distance who this young woman was, for, to be sure, she was his own daughter in disguise—a girl who had been born to him decades after the departure of his fierce and once-loyal champion. She had left the court of her father to explore the world and see what it might offer to her, but being of royal blood, she had not fared as well as the rough berserker had done—if one can say that the life of a beggar is faring well. As the King approached the two companions, he smiled and held his hands out to both of them. *Come home*, he called with tears in his eyes. *It's time to come home.*'

1

Don Luan

I moved to L.A. in mid-1988 for a girl, but when that didn't work out the way we had both hoped (it rarely ever does), I decided to stay—or at least *thought* I decided. I had no idea at the time that it was really a coven of sorcerers I had moved there to see—or, better said, to interact with.

I met Donald Luan just after I moved into the Regency, an apartment building which used to sit on North Orange Drive a half block north of Hollywood Boulevard, two buildings behind the Chinese Theatre, and a half block south of the Magic Castle where all the magicians hang out, and I believe some even make their homes.

Don lived on the second floor of the Regency, like I did, but near the end of the dimly-lit, musty hallway at the back of the unkempt once-regal building. This old structure had been home to Bogie and Marilyn Monroe, and maybe countless other stars since the 1940s—or so Don informed me. After nearly two decades of talks to get rid of it, the Regency was razed to the ground sometime after 2002 to make way for yet another parking lot. *Hooray for Hollywood!*

About a week after I moved in, Bob Haggard, the on-site building manager who I once found sitting in the musty old chair in my apartment when I came home from work because, he explained, he liked the feel of my place, gave me a book, and asked me to read it. He wanted to know what I thought about it. I already had my thoughts about *him*, but I decided not to tell him what they were. Anyway, the book was about something called *brujeria*, and was written by some guy named Arlo Costanada. I told Bob that I had lots of reading time, which I did. As I delved into the easy if paradigm-challenging read, I wasn't particularly struck by the writing, which was both sub-par and painfully reiterative. I did find, though, that I detested the subject of the thesis; this so-called *brujeria* or sorcery which was far from being anything similar to the wisdom I had grown up with—which would be my empirical point of reference, of course. The book was filled with wildly fantastic fiction passed off as fact. For example, not many people actively seek out sorceresses who can transform into hirsute tangles of growling, tumbling snarl. From the first few pages of the book, I saw right through the whole thing as being nothing other than a Southwest version of witchcraft *a la* Endor,[1] which I hated with a perfect hatred.

My new buddy Don soon told me about a woman called Ensueña who also lived in Hollywood. She was a colleague of the beguiling self-styled *brujo*, or male witch, Arlo Costanada. With fierce eyes that at the same time, oddly, exuded a powerful kindness, Don added that Ensueña had become, since her own fairly recent initiation into the coven, the skeleton key to the path of brujeria they followed and practiced—a position which had always been held by the most powerful *dreamer* in the coven—a *dreamer* being the opposite of a *stalker*. Strange terminology, I thought, for *pensive* and *outgoing*—respectively. Don told me that if I could succeed in pulling Ensueña out and away from the keyhole, so to speak, and 'lose' her, as with any other key, this 1960s-fabricated line of New Age witchcraft would fall apart—and not only that, but would begin to disintegrate and eventually become as if it had never existed. How did an old man who lived alone in an unkempt Hollywood building know all this? Well, he said he had studied their cult for years, praying unceasingly about it, and God was showing him things about various spiritual wars being fought over Los Angeles and its residents. This city, he added, had, because of film and television, become *the* hub-city of the world. Okay. Not a problem. I didn't have anything better to do than to singlehandedly destroy a method of witchcraft branded internationally as the perfect postmodern concept of reality—hyped as the only path known on Earth that would ever lead to true freedom for its followers. This was, of course, as long as they gave heed to the number 42, a figure for which no one could remember the importance.[2]

Don stood to stretch his legs. 'How do you like the paperback our friendly property manager Bob Haggard loaned you, Bastion? Anything interesting in it?'

'You know about him giving a book to me?'

---

[1] I Samuel 28.7

[2] A cursory glance through the Bible will show clearly that 42 is the number of ill omen.

'I know a few things, yeah. But only what God tells me, or one of his angels. Winged creatures and all that. They like to tell the secrets of us imprudent humans.'[1]

I cleared my throat. Something felt caught in it. Los Angeles smog or something. 'Alright then, Don. Tell me what Arlo Costanada is about, in your own mind—or maybe what God has told you.'

'Alright, let's see. Arlo Costanada is a self-licking lollipop who claims, for whatever reason, to be the inheritor of a specific sorcery lineage that spans generations—a lineage of which he has asserted himself to be the last, and final, leader. The man's world exists primarily in the books that he authors—all of which say pretty much the same thing over and over. Human Development expert Yusuf Hilton Peace has stated that Costanada's mentor John Matanza is the most important icon of paradigm shift since Jesus. Interesting statement, if utterly untrue. Essentially, Costanada likes causing all kinds of trouble and getting rich in the process.

I felt my face go hot with anger at the belligerent affront of these super-spiritual jackasses. They claimed themselves to be so wise but proved themselves, in the long run, to be sheer idiots. Or, maybe they were just ultra-slick snake oil salesmen. Whatever the case, I found them appalling.

Don looked into my eyes with the kindness of a loving grandfather. 'Bastion, resilience of the duped is the common response among those who follow the witchy path of that silly so-called 'sorcerer', just so you know ahead of time. That same sort of comment, by the way, is a common attack against Christianity, in case you aren't aware, that never holds an ounce of water simply because every true Believer from the Crucifixion forward has met Jesus personally—because he has revealed himself to them—and spends quality time with him, and receives his miracles of healing and transformation and life abundant—something Gautama Buddha and Krishna and Odin and the Tao and the imaginary John Matanza cannot do, though they all may promise as much. And every true Believer from the Crucifixion backward to Adam knew and, because of God's revelation of himself, spent quality time with the Living Word and Spirit of El Elyon, and received his glory and

---

[1] Ecclesiastes 10.20

presence in their lives—something Baal Peor and Moloch and Dagon and Chemosh and Athena and Zeus and the rest—gods of wood and stone—could not bring to anybody. Mention the name of Buddha or Krishna or Moroni and his buddy Joseph Smith and unbelievers shrug and sometimes make complimentary comments about dedication and religious effort to overcome social sorrows. But mention Jesus and they cringe and often become violent. Why is this, if, as they say, he was just another man? Why such inner turmoil to the mere name of *just another man*? Anyway, Bastion, here's one for you. Why do demons never possess lawyers?'

I shook my head. Now Don was telling me a joke? 'I don't know, man. Why don't demons possess lawyers?'

'Professional courtesy.'

♪

I was young. I certainly didn't feel prepared to take on a toxic flight[1] of witches—especially ones whose many, many followers—because of the wide distribution of Costanada's books—declared that it didn't even matter if there was a John Matanza or a line of sorcery or not because Costanada had in fact discovered *the* missing link to the human problem; the way out of all the pain into an infinitude of personal freedom. I told Don my thoughts on the whole thing, and asked him why he had never confronted the witches himself. He replied that he had once, but in his own strength, not God's. As a result, the sorcerers had given him quite a thrashing. It took him a good stretch of time, he confessed, to recover from their ferocious counterattack. He slid up the short sleeves of his Panama shirt and showed me the insides of his upper arms. It was as if they had been clawed from just above the elbows to the armpits by talons as sharp as razors. 'Down my back, too, from my neck to my lumbar,' he added. 'Pretty painful. These sorcerers come across in public as highly evolved spiritual beings, until you invade their fortress, as it were. God allowed them to discipline me because of my acting outside of his will in the matter and trying to trounce them in my own power, like the sons of

---

[1] coven

Sceva did.[1] You have to go in the spirit of the Torn Veil, Bastion, or don't go at all, son. Don't go at all. But no worries. You have angels stationed all around you, son.'

I felt repulsed by what I had read, and now had also heard, about the witches. This was all just too much! I asked Don why he thought I was any better prepared to confront them than he had been? He said that he could *see* better now than he could back in the day, and the minute I moved to the Regency, he knew I was a specific answer to his prayer. What was his prayer? That God would send warriors more powerful than any of the sorcerers in the system he hated so much. He wasn't so much concerned, he said, with the *brujos* and *brujas* involved in traditional Indian and Mexican witchcraft, or the practitioners of Santeria, Voudon, Vodou, Candomblé, and La Santa Muerte, or even the *lechuzas* or owl-witches and the like. All of them, he added, garnered support through the embarrassing failure of Christendom[2] in their various Afro-Indian-Latin based cultures, but the *real* danger, he insisted, was the wide dissemination of Arlo Costanada books—in short, the pop-culturing of witchcraft for the masses comparable to what Gerald Gardner had been able to accomplish with those of a more European kinship a decade or so before Costanada came on the scene here in the West. 'But that jackanapes is missing one key element,' Don added. 'Costanada skips the camaraderie that Gardnerians and other witches enjoy with one another. Instead, he insists on secrecy and quirkiness as his *modus operandi* in much the same way as do the Neo-Gnostics who, of course, claim that anybody who calls himself a *Gnostic* proves that he is not one. Just more New Age trip-trap. Anyway, Costanada insists that impeccability, or perfection, is accomplished first by a person before any of the magical qualities and gifts of life—or Infinity as he calls it—open and present themselves for the taking. That's really off-putting seeing that human beings can't even truly love the ones they care for the most without divine assistance, but still there are hundreds of thousands of people hungering for magical lives whose paths have been drastically altered by this charlatan's out-and-out

---

[1] Acts 19.11-20

[2] Another term, coined by Kierkegaard, for organized religion as opposed to the real relationship with God known as *Christianity*.

lies—and quite a few of them have been completely destroyed in the process. It's all unconscionable and immoral, and the man has to be stopped—or, in the very least, people have to be warned. What I see happening is a death—some kind of death of the inner circle eventually, and then a slow disintegration of Costanada's organization to the point that it becomes just any other California weird religious association that offers yoga, feel-good meditation, inside-info lectures, martial arts classes, and quirky private jokes and stories to tell at those gay Hollywood parties.'

Don's last words hit my funny bone. I laughed. The levity was good for the heavy moment. I felt like something that was gripping me let go—a fear or, as I have said, a revulsion to the whole picture being painted by my new friend. 'So what next, Don? I just go and introduce myself to this woman Ensueña and tell her that I've arrived to destroy her and all her witch friends? That she's their skeleton key and I'm there to pull her out of the keyhole and then lose her?'

'Well,' replied Don, 'that's pretty much what I did with the original key La Mora, and it got me nowhere. False bravado never does. Anyway, I don't think you'll have to go looking for Ensueña, since I believe she'll come looking for you.'

I stepped back and studied Don. Because I had to get to the bank before they closed for the day, I stood in the musty old hallway of the Regency. Don leaned in the doorway of his room, almost nonchalant in his air. His straight, thick salt-n-pepper hair was messed up and he was unshaven for at least two days, yet his body looked lean and agile for a man his age—I guessed about 60 or so. He had been a good-looking guy in his prime, I could see, and he still held a certain *savoir-faire* that I felt must have been the reason people were drawn to him. *I* was after all drawn to him, but I gave myself room to realize, at this point in my life, that I was drawn to anybody and everybody for every reason under the sun—even psychic vampires I knew were such but wanted to break open to see what made them tick. I didn't see the world as my oyster—my perception of who I was wasn't strong enough yet, and I also despised the idea of stepping on heads to get what I wanted, which I knew was the Hollywood way to do things. Aquatically speaking, I was a sponge. Everybody had something to teach me, I didn't care who it was or how they taught it as long as I was in no danger, physical or otherwise, during the process. I loved people and wanted to be around them as much as possible—even the bad guys. If they posed a threat, I moved on. If they didn't, we became friends should they want to be, because I had the time if they did. Hollywood was, and still is, filled with people of every personality, every ideal possible, every walk of life, every perversity, and, believe it or not, every morality. That probably goes for Los Angeles in general, but Hollywood is the maraschino cherry on top of the ice cream soda. The *suicide* ice cream soda, that is.[1]

The first job I landed was on Melrose Avenue, at a high-end Space Age-themed 'gourmet' t-shirt shop called Vacationland where, in '88, a screen-printed t-shirt cost an alarming $20.[2] We sold over a hundred different rotating designs, and daily hosted at least one celebrity who had meandered in off the avenue to have a look around, and maybe even buy something. Three or four of us ran the place at a time, and we worked well together, few conflicts, just experiencing Hollywood for what it was at the time—a dirty, exciting, decrepit city filled with lies and life and dashed dreams. Sweet are my memories of the precious people I met, talked with, spent quality time with. I lift up a prayer for each one of them whenever I remember them, because it's never the place that's important, it's the people in the place— the people who touch our lives in a wide variety of ways, whatever their faults may be, whatever their desires, however they can love—even if it's just one soft word or an act of kindness. One little word, one little action, goes a long, long way in Hollywood, California—the world of contrast between the place left behind and the place discovered. There the ever-present sham architecture is seen as metaphor of the absence of artistic control as well as symbol of the last frontier of the American Dream turned so quickly to nightmare. Thus was born the 'Los Angeles Anti-Myth'— Southern California as the place of the fresh start as well as the scene of the disastrous finish. Watch the classic Noir film *Sunset Boulevard* for a finer point on the idea.

---

[1] A *suicide* is a mixture of all the available options at a soda fountain, including the diet versions.

[2] The nicest screen-print tees of that era were never more than 10 dollars, still being expensive since minimum wage was no more than $4.00 after taxes.

2

Ronaldo

I'm fond of the writing style of James Herriot, if not of all his content. If, for example, you know his book *The Lord God Made Them All*, then you'll see some reflection of his style in this book—as well as some Hemingway and maybe a few other writers. Anyway, if you don't know Herriot, he mixes up times and dates chapter to chapter, and includes journal entries from decades before as chapters in and of themselves. As his reader, I am not asked to follow one line of thinking through an entire book cover to cover. I can stop with Herriot after a chapter and digest it for a day or two before moving forward, or backwards in time. So, really, each of his chapters is its own short story, and this, for me, makes for interesting, and relaxing, reading. But don't get too comfortable with my own work. I'm not a pastoral Yorkshire veterinarian from the middle of the 20th Century who writes cute stories about happy children and contented cows and their farmers. I'm a monster-hunter born during the Vietnam War, and born to do battle—quite like a berserker— yet not against flesh and blood, but with the proverbial 'forces of evil,' being principalities, powers, and rulers of the darkness of this world system. Sounds too fantastic to be true? Well, if that's the case, then your local library will have a copy of a Herriot book if you need something a little lighter in nature—or *about* nature.

No, I wasn't about to become a disgruntled David and don unrealistic armor to go out and do battle with the Goliath who stood before me during his intermission from taunting the righteous and keeping them enslaved to Dagon. If I was to be commissioned by Don Luan to meet Ensueña and cohorts face to face, then I would go in the Spirit of the God I had served from early childhood, or I wouldn't go at all. I was young and fearless, but any might or power I held was not my own, I knew, and I rested in the confidence and peace that this knowledge brought to me. Being young—in my mid-twenties—I had a wide variety of interests, most of them, as I have said, quite human. The old gorgeously- crafted buildings of Hollywood, the rich (if brief) history of

Tinseltown,[1] the flurry of Filmland activity, the music and club scenes, the themed house parties, were all only backdrops—some not so nice after all the glitz and glamour wore off—for the beautiful people I met and loved, if they would let me. Many didn't, but it's a big city, and if I saw them again at all, it was always for a reason—and sometimes that reason was for them to have their love tested yet again, just like mine was being tested.

'No,' said Don as he handed me a warm homemade chocolate chip cookie, 'you wouldn't introduce yourself as a monster-hunting Christian. That would be the wrong tack with a nest of potent witches who despise Jesus. If you did that, you might find yourself in the same boat as the proverbial 'seven sons of Sceva' who had their asses kicked by a demon-possessed man who saw right through their utter lack of command and their attempt to use the 'Jesus of Saint Paul' as a magical exorcism spell. Hey, we all make mistakes, dude. But some of our mistakes can be downright comical. Mine, for instance.'

Don had called me *dude*. I was from Northwest Florida. It wasn't in our vocabulary. The only time most West Floridians ever even heard the word was when *Grand Funk Railroad* came on one of the local AOR[2] FM radio stations with their song 'We're An American Band.' This common noun *dude* was weird to hear, but I found it even weirder to be called one—even though my Uncle Hulon, born in Flora-Bama in 1920, had always called me *dude*. But somehow this had never counted. Anyway, when Don Luan called me *dude*, it wasn't the first time since I had been in Hollywood, but I had only been there a little while, so the word was still fresh—and I certainly wasn't using it myself yet. When I later tried it out at the bookstore, where I got a job a week or so I left the t-shirt shop, after having cut my chops on every street in Hollywood I could get my feet on, so to speak,

---

[1] In 1910, D. W. Griffith directs the first film shot in Hollywood, *In Old California*, because of the friendly small-town population and the beautiful location.

[2] Album Oriented Rock, a radio format developed in the late 1960's and directed at the Baby Boomer generation. The Classic Rock format was later designed to replicate the AOR format for nostalgic Boomers.

The Teachings of Don Luan

Ronaldo Yunque, a good friend from Marin County[1], strongly objected to the word *dude* and said he preferred his name, or at least 'man.' I still called him 'dude' after that. I believed he had finally gotten used to it after a while, but when for Christmas he bought me a grey Confederate soldier cap because, he said, my people were from 'Alabamy,' I figured that he had never gotten over being referred to as either a New Yorker visiting the Wild West or a streetwise rock-n-roller—a *dude*. Truth was, Ronaldo was a real mystery. He enjoyed the allegedly more moral 1910s through the early 1960s as his choice of eras which lent themselves to his speech, manner, and conservative hair and clothing style. Yet, being anti-war across the board, he had firmly adopted not only the nonviolence of the Flower Children of his pre-teen years in San Francisco, but their damnable social concept known as 'political correctness' which, as it turns out, only supports those who also adopt the PC lifestyle believing that relativity—live and let live—is the only viable reality for mankind, and that anybody standing for any idea which seems to ostracize any other group is not politically correct and should be ostracized for their stupidity and, of course, slowness of evolution while keeping us all entrenched in the scratch-and-claw fight for survival. Liberalism is based in the idea that morality is only an evolutionary survival tactic that keeps us out of wars and other potentially deadly conflicts. There's nothing wrong with tolerance of others we don't agree with. Truth is, that's the only way the Light can reveal itself for the love and acceptance that it actually is. But there is something inherently evil about an intolerance of those who hold *peacefully* to the idea that morality is a conscious and individual response to the cosmic law of harmony and equality while refusing relativity and evolution as outright lies which breed inequality. And those who promote 'PC' are most guilty of this 'intolerance of the intolerant,' because, according to their *Weltanschauung*, everybody is right—unless of course a person happens to believe that there is only one Way out of this colossal mess, that being the Living Word manifested in Jesus of Nazareth. Then that same person being gang raped and then run over by a speeding train isn't a good enough punishment, because he has upset their delicate *lebensraum* and their precious

---

[1] A wealthy county in the San Francisco Bay Area.

PC—their Final Solution designed to rid the world of those who gear their lives toward a conscious obedience to the law of harmony which, of course, must come from a Lawgiver— the very idea causing Liberals to cringe and gnash their teeth. It is impossible to understand the politics of the godless mind without grasping that it is all about *deniable intimidation*. Still, even though PC was only a mask that Ronaldo wore over his generally moral soul, I loved him, and he and I are actually still in touch today, though it's been nearly three decades since we last spent time with one another. I did make him laugh until he cried the day before he was traditionally married, when he graciously phoned to tell me the happy news. That was the best gift I could give him, I reckon, for the true friendship that he had given me— though he was often shocked by me, and even put out with me every once in a blue moon.

3

Jennifer

I asked Don, after I had rudely awakened him from a mid-afternoon nap by banging on his door, how I was supposed to prepare myself for this conflict with the witches.

'Well, you could start by giving a listen to the lyrics of musician Rich Mullins.'

'Never heard of him.'

'You've heard his songs though. Believe me. Anyway, Bastion, the time of Man is closing, so just do your thing, dude. Keep working at the t-shirt shop, keep staying in top shape on that crazy mountain bike of yours, and keep being friends with that sweetheart Rachael, because she needs you as her friend, she sees you as a solid rock in this untoward floodland. Do you see many other bikes in Hollywood, or many people walking? Of course you don't. This city travels on four fat rubber wheels for the most part, my man. Ray Bradbury found that out a long, long time ago, in Venice I believe it was, when he and a buddy of his were pulled over by the police just for walking down a sidewalk.'

'Yeah, I remember reading something about that and how he wrote *Fahrenheit 451* because of it. I like Bradbury.'

'So do I. He's pure godless in some stories, though—back to that relativity thing again, which he seems to embrace. Anyway, you'll know when you're supposed to meet Ensueña, or the other sorcerers, or all of them together—which would be quite a show, I have to say!'

'How in the world, Don, have you somehow convinced me that my move to Hollywood was so that I could take down a secret witchcraft coven like Attorney Johnson took down Capone? Am I insane? Wait. Are *you* insane?'

Don's smile was warm. His eyes glimmered in the nearly nonexistent hall light aided only by two small windows, one at either end of the building three times as long as it was wide. (As an aside, the windows for each first floor room, or apartment, were too high off the ground to be entered without a ladder. Evidently the architect had believed in security.)

I looked down at my scuffed black combat boots with their bright yellow laces. They looked great against the faded, stained red carpet. Of course there would be red carpet in a

building built for starlets. What else? The light we had for
extra illumination of the old joint found some of its way
down to me and Don from a creepy old haunted-house-
looking chandelier that only held five burning bulbs out of a
possible nine. I smelled bacon cooking in somebody else's
room, and the XXX album by the crazed band *Jane's
Addiction* blared up from a first floor room—likely played by
one of the six or seven young longhair Rockers who lived at
the Regency. I liked that moment a lot.

'I'm starting to believe that I've convinced you of nothing,
Bastion. You say you came out to Hollywood for a girl, right?
A Christian girl?'

'*Very* Christian—the most Christian anybody can be. Her
name's Jennifer.'

'Oh yes. I know her.'

I was naive as all get out at this point in my life, but I
hadn't just fallen off the cabbage truck the day before. I
sighed. 'This is Hollywood, Don. Her name is Jennifer. The
most common girl name in my generation. And, she lives in
Orange County. How could you possibly know her?'

'Jennifer Cooper, right?'

I rocked back on my heels. 'Wild, wild guess is all.'

'Alright then. Jennifer *Marie* Cooper. Goes by Jenny
Peacechild? She's tall, thin, has kinky auburn hair, wears
combat boots like you do, is sweet and soft-spoken, and
attends Pacific Christian College. Better?'

I stepped back in near apoplexy. 'How did—?'

'Bastion. Surely you know what I am by now.' As Don
spoke, he leaned his face against the door-frame so that all of
his nose showed but only one side of his mouth moved while
he talked. The result was hilarious. He seemed to enjoy
making me laugh. He kept doing it. As I laughed, I thought,
What a ridiculously funny cartoon this would make! To
make things even better, he lowered his voice a couple of
octaves and added a raspy, gravelly effect that made him
sound a lot like Nick Nolte.

Most people, when they are trying to exert their authority
to someone they view as inferior to themselves, say things
like 'Don't you know *who* I am?' or 'Do you know *who* you
are talking to?' The word 'who' denotes a personality as well
as a vain attempt at singularity and hierarchic power. But no.
Don asked me if I knew *what* he was. 'What' denotes a kind
or a type, a work or a purpose for existence, yet only a cog in
the wheel of the bigger machine. 'What' sidetracks vanity and

allows its user to step into timeless eternity as an important piece of the cosmic gestalt.

'I think I *might* know what you are. But help me. I'll probably need your help on this one, Don.'

The old man closed his eyes. 'Elisha, the prophet who is in Israel, tells the king of Israel the words that you speak in your bedchamber.'

I recognized the Bible scripture immediately. From II Kings 6. 'A prophet. You're a prophet. You know things.'

'I do, yes, Bastion. But I take no glory for myself. I love God with all of my heart, all of my soul, all of my mind, and all of my strength. In this way I can love myself—finally, after all these years of pain and struggle—and when that is happening, I can, and do, love others, despite what they say or do, which is an impossibility if we are not in moment-to-moment communion with our Creator. Love has no boundaries. Love reaches out from its Source—the Living Word—and teaches, instructs, encourages, inspires, fills us with security and, yes, gives vision. Sometimes love even scares the hell out of people. I like that aspect too. It's harmless fun.'

'So, you know Jennifer?'

'Yep. And she knows me. We even enjoyed a delicious lunch together one time at Gorky's on Cahuenga. Good coffee, too.'

♪

Right after I moved to Hollywood and got my place at the Regency, Jennifer drove up one Friday night from the 'Orange Curtain,' as we all called the county situated just below Los Angeles—making reference to the ultra-conservative aspect of that county many people compared to the USSR with its 'Iron Curtain.' Anyway, Jennifer and I spent that chilly late-May evening on Melrose Avenue between La Brea and Fairfax Avenues—the hipper (and less dangerous) section of the strip. As we strolled, I was given the chance to see the beauty of Christ in Jennifer as she suffered for his Name, and I will never forget it. We were walking by one of the nameless Hardcore Punk Rock clothing stores—not quite vintage yet since that music era was less than a decade old—when the owner or manager or somebody stuck her head out to have a cigarette or something and Jennifer recognized her and stopped to ask her if she'd like to have another stack of xeroxed *Deferent Dreamer* magazines for her store—a free monthly Xian Underground 'zine[1] Jennifer edited and published with her own money. It featured lots of Post-Punk poetry (some I had written myself), artwork, and album and live show reviews, all Christ-centered, all super hip and up-to-the-minute.

The store manager's face screwed up and turned a furious reddish-purple. 'Fuck you! I remember you! *No!* No more of your freaky Jesus Creep bullshit in my store! You hear me, girl? Get the fuck away from me!'

Wow. *That* stung. I said nothing. Jennifer was visibly hurt. Her naturally pale and freckled face turned pink as she cast her eyes to the nasty sidewalk as we strolled along. She never mentioned one word about the incident. But I knew her. Maybe not as well as Don knew her, or God knew her in his all-encompassing love and knowing, but I knew her well enough to understand that she didn't take the occurrence to heart—*her* heart, anyway. No. She took it to the heart of Jesus, and laid it there, and let him heal her. He did. One day he healed her so completely that he took her home to be with him forever.

I miss Jennifer, but I know that I will see her again one day, and I will be able to personally thank her for making herself available to be used to change the entire trajectory of my life, and therefore the lives of many others. Her love for me, her caring for me—and maybe even prophetically— helped to develop me into a berserker for the Kingdom.

Here's one of my poems Jennifer published in the very next issue of *Deferent Dreamer*:

Ancient secrets now revealed
to the one who truly feels,
truly loves, and truly tries;
verily, the one who dies,
first for Christ, then for all kin;
then that small circle within

---

[1] The 'Christian Underground' was a maga*zine*-and-cassette disseminated pop-culture movement which began in about 1985 and fizzled out within the following decade. The person who coined the name was a 'zine publisher (*Darc Colours*) and poet by the name of Scottie Joel Cooper, whereabouts today unknown.

daily walk and circumspect;
then unknown, unwanted vets
of this war known as The Fall;
beaten, torn; we see them all
the time; do we truly care
for eyes glowing with hating stares?
Give it up or throw it in.
Fight this war or love your sin.
Years I've cried 'The line is drawn!
Middle ground has long since gone!'

4

Badehaus

'Where exactly in L.A. does Ensueña live, Don?'

'She lives right here in Hollywood.'

'Where? Sunset? Santa Monica? Melrose? Here on the Boulevard? Vine? Up north of Franklin? Argyle maybe? Vista Del Mar?'

'I see you've been riding your bike on your days off.'

'Yeah, and I love it too. So, where do I find her? I mean, when I'm ready for that step. Knocking keys out of keyholes and stuff.'

'She'll likely find you first, so relax. By the way, one of the other witches has a pad not far from where we're standing, truth be told.'

We were standing at Don's threshold, me in the hallway and him leaning up against some part of his doorway—the door itself or the doorframe. Just then the door to the apartment across from Don opened. A gorgeous Eurasian woman who looked to be in her mid-30s looked out and gave us both a weak smile. By the bleary look of her pretty 'slanted' eyes, we had apparently awakened her from an afternoon nap. Her physique was slight but athletic. I noticed that her hair was cut to her shoulders but had been left long enough for a short ponytail—typical of women who are sports minded so they can still pull their hair up when they jog or work out, play tennis or whatever they do. She closed her door as softly as she had opened it.

'I haven't met that lady yet, Don.'

'You will. *Eventually.*'

'Who is she?'

'I'd rather let the Angelenos tell their own stories. It's more fun that way, don't you think? I wouldn't want anybody else telling mine, would you?'

'I'm a writer, Don. I tell other people's stories all the time, whether they know it or not. They usually don't.'

'Never make a writer mad, eh Bastion?' Don quipped as he lit up a cig.

'You smoke?'

'Nah. It's just for effect. What's Hollywood without smooth talk, a coffin nail, and a glass of poison?'

'Okay, dude, I'll catch you later. Gotta head up to *Ralph's* for some milk and ramen. Maybe a can of tuna. Get you anything?'

'Sounds like you eat about like I do. *Simple.*'

'I have to. Otherwise I wouldn't have rent money.'

'That bad, hoh? Oh, would you get me a gallon of regular horchata? Not the strawberry kind.'[1] He pulled a ten out of his slacks pocket, handed it to me, told me to keep the change, waved goodbye, and then went back inside his apartment. I heard him singing an old hymn—*Softly and Tenderly Jesus Is Calling*—one of my favorites from childhood. I stood in the hallway a few seconds. I turned around and gazed at the quiet woman's door, half hoping she might come back, maybe introduce herself, ask me who I was—tell me about her life. She was extremely attractive to me, but I knew I had to be sober and vigilant. Hollywood was filled to the brim with that kind of magnetism, and a thousand others besides. If I slipped, my light would go out, and then what would be the point of my living in the City of Lights?

I had to go back in my unlocked apartment to get my wallet. In my entire history of renting apartments—a long and checkered one, to be sure—I have never had a doorknob lock so cantankerous as the one at the Regency. When I first moved in, it too me three or four minutes to get the thing open. Then I was stopped one night by Rufus, who I'll talk more about later, who warned me that I'd better learn how to open my door a lot faster than I was because what if I was being chased and needed quick sanctuary? I took his advice and became a lot more intimate with my contentious door than I had been before Rufus threw me into the middle of a murder mystery or crime drama.

When I flipped the kitchen light on to see how much tuna I needed, the work area next to the icebox[2] changed color from a coffee brown to its normal eggshell white. *Roaches.* Hundreds of them. I didn't know about boric acid at the time, and even if I had, would the grocery store have had it for sale? Would I have even been able to afford it? The flea

---

[1] A refreshing Mexican drink made of rice, milk, vanilla, and cinnamon—and sometimes also flavored with strawberry juice.

[2] refrigerator

infestation a month later—because of the downstairs drug dealer's side project of breeding puppies in a dog box outside his window directly below my own screenless window was only taken care of by a care package from my aging parents in Pensacola who, upon request, sent me several branches of the mercury plant. I promptly crushed the leaves which had dried in cross-continent transit and spread them all over my revolting, ripped avocado-green carpet. The fleas left immediately and never came back, but the puppies kept me awake at night with their yapping, at least until the druggie— who was Rufus himself—decided the animals weren't worth the trouble and got rid of them somehow. Sold them or something, since I wasn't aware of any lakes in the general area.

As I rode my bicycle the little over a half mile to the grocery store on Sunset Boulevard—*Ralph's*—I asked God to protect me and keep me safe, keep his warrior angels around me at every turn. Just as I wheeled into the parking lot, a silver Saab swung around but didn't see me. I hit the guy head on. He wasn't moving fast, but I shot up on my front wheel and sort of went over the handle bars without actually letting them go—but bending them sideways. The driver sat still for a second and then slowly got out, panic written all over his face. He was cleanly shaven, dressed to the nines, and sported an immaculate haircut with a sharply coiffured nape, but also wore a telling silver loop through his septum.

'My god! Are you alright man?' His eyes were bugging out. 'Are you hurt?'

'Yeah, I'm alright,' I said as I quickly scanned the damage to his expensive car. 'I'm sorry.'

'Oh my god it's *my* fault! You okay? You *sure* you okay?' He raced around to where I stood. I dismounted, clenched my front tire between my knees, and wrenched the handlebars back into semi-working order. He pulled a business card from a shiny, fat leather wallet. It said *Bruce Badehaus*, and below that *District Manager, Brentano's Bookstores*, then fax and phone numbers. That's when he saw the deep, two foot scratch torn into the hood of the vehicle that had set him back 30 Grand. His face went from a frightened white to a furious purple as he looked from me to his hood, back to me, then his hood, then back to me. His former words of compassion gave way to accusative expletives as he fell back into the driver's seat, slammed the door, and raced away. I didn't feel bad at all about the incident. I was in the right-of-way, but of course upper level management in their Saabs, especially of his particular nose-hoop-wearing variety, have the final say in Hollywood, even if it's only a few cuss words. Gratefully, I found a bike rack unseen from the supermarket parking lot and locked up with my handy-dandy U-lock. That way if Badehaus came back to exact revenge on my poor horse, at least I wouldn't have to walk back home. I had bought groceries at this store on foot before, but it hadn't been any fun at all toting the green Army duffel bag my brother-in-law Mel had given me, filled with cans of tomato soup and v*eg-all* mixed vegetables. I had to have that kind of food to go with my ramen and peanut butter and grape jelly so I wouldn't develop canker sores in my mouth, which used to happen all the time when all I ate was pizza, fries, pasta salad, and burgers on Melrose Avenue—when I could actually *afford* that kind of food.

There are all kinds of monsters in the world, the hobbyhorse Saab driver being of the relatively harmless variety—unless, of course, he demands that my angelic visitors be sent out into the night to be used as his sexual playthings. Then the game changes pretty drastically, and people can pretty much expect a divinely-inspired conflagration at that point. I realized, even at my youthful age, that I wasn't made to challenge every sort of fiend out there. Don, I knew, had in no way coerced me, but had only provided needed confirmation to what I already realized every time I was in a record store and came across a copy of any recording by the band *Christian Death*. I was a postmodern witch-hunter, and with God's help I would not fail. Without his help, though, I was dead meat in the freezer for some maniac's candlelit dinner for two. Yes, I had seen the film *Manhunter*. Yes, it had scared me silly.

5

Stickman

I failed the whole shebang, of course. So terribly, in fact, that, to retaliate against myself for my foolishness, I moved back to Northwest Florida—specifically Frangista Beach—to work with the infamous monk-priest Euseb Pappastephanou who had relocated there from Wisconsin to build yet another Greek Orthodox church five miles from where two others sat within a mile of one another. But this move—this venture—only made my life worse and me more bitter than I already was, so after seven months of living an extremely lonely life on a deserted NW Florida beach (Frangista, now called Miramar) in a vintage Airstream trailer (bathroom with no place to take a bath, tiny bed, miniscule kitchen with full-size fridge, full couch) and doing things my way instead of God's way, I headed back to Hollywood and a much lower paying bookstore job (not, thankfully, managed by Bruce Badehaus), and this time I hoped I was ready for my work in the City. I found nothing had changed at the Regency. Everybody who had lived there before was still living there, and they all greeted me as if I was a lost puppy they had found. I got hugs from the guys and pecks on the cheek from the girls—most of whom were low-level prostitutes, preferring to be called 'groupies,' who had moved in on the game without a pimp. Lots of business in Hollywood. Nobody sweats a few freelancers doing what they do.

♪

I hadn't been back in Tinseltown for more than two weeks before I met a mild-mannered Skinhead called Stickman. I was standing on Melrose Avenue not too far from Poinsettia Place on of my two days off from work when he walked up to me and held his thin hand out in a gesture of friendship.
'Oi! They call me Stickman. It fits, don't ya think?'
His grey eyes were kind, if not a little bleary—as if he had been awake all night, or maybe several days and nights. I smiled and took his clammy hand. 'I'm Bastion. Cool to meet ya, dude.' (This may have been my first use of the dreaded word, actually.)

'You ever tricked, Bastion?' he asked me with a bluntness that rolled me back on my heels. 'I'm a chicken. I trick for a livin'.'

'Have I ever done *what*?' I was still interested in all kinds of people, and I knew what a chicken was. My uncle, my mother's brother, had warned me about possibly becoming a chicken for lack of anything better to do in L.A., or for lack of food and shelter—whichever came first. *Chicken: A male prostitute who hooks their tricks (acquires their customers) by sitting at bus stops after city bus route hours.* A black expensive car actually stopped for me late one night while I was waiting for the last bus home, but sped away—embarrassed, I guess—when I didn't run over to his window to seal the deal and get in. Then, on top of that, the last bus of the night passed me even though I was standing and waving like a lover saying goodbye to her ill-fated soldier boy.

I was 'open' to people. As I've said, I had never seen much of anything. I was wary, though. I would only let people take me so far, and then I'd jump off. I was *naturally* streetwise, you might say. I believe it's how I survived the rough neighborhoods of Hollywood. Well, that and guardian angels watching over me like mama bears watch over their young.

'Yeah,' Stickman continued as if on cue. 'But I do it a little different than a lot of the guys. I tell the old dude, lawyer or whatever—banker, maybe—that I'm only into S&M, and *he* has to play the masochist.'[1]

I was intrigued, though I really didn't want to be. 'So what happens?' I heard myself ask, and then I was sorry.

'Well,' Stickman began with obvious relish, licking his thin lips with a long pinkish-white tongue. I could see disease all over it. I stepped away a foot. Then I got a whiff of his noxious breath. Peppermint and old flu mixed together. 'Wanna mouth freshener?' he asked as his fingers dove into his tight faded jeans pocket and fished out a roll of mints—which were accompanied by pocket lint, an assortment of loose change, a crumpled condom (still in its packet, thank heaven), a wad of twine, and a worn-out dollar bill.

'No thanks,' I replied. I regretted shaking Stickman's hand. I wiped my fingers on my vintage Vietnam War

---

[1] The receiver of the sexual pain, the giver being the *sadist*.

camouflage pants. He didn't seem to take any notice to my discomfort, and continued.

'Well anyway,' he continued, 'like last night for instance. I hooked this exec and after I convinced him that S&M was the only way he was gonna get pleasure from me, he took me back to his plush rental pad on Sunset. See, I carry strong cord with me and everything. I tied that mofo up and proceeded to demonstrate my abilities. Then I put my pants back on, gagged him with a terrycloth washrag and some duct tape, picked up his Rolex and his fat wallet, and just walked out, him tryin' his damnedest to scream at me to untie him. I just laughed and disappeared. I do this kind of stuff all the time. Only rarely will I actually have sex, and that's always with a hot woman. I like the older women. You like women or men?' He turned his wrist to look at the time, and sure enough he was wearing a gold Rolex. '12:15,' he said as if talking to somebody else.

'Women,' I replied, stunned.

'Older or younger?'

I didn't want to answer. To me, it would sound perverted either way.

'That's alright. Keep it to yourself. You know why I'm talkin' to you?'

'Not really,' I replied with as much nonchalance as I could muster. I was afraid of his answer.

'Because I'm not scared of *nothin'*, man. Not even 'Rude Boys' like yourself. In fact, I've discovered that if I talk to dudes everybody else is scared of, they usually turn out to be pretty nice people.'

I swelled up at his words. I had seen *The Clash* film 'Rude Boy,' but I wasn't making the connection. Did I look like somebody people were scared of? *Hmmm*— maybe I did. This was a real plus on the mean streets of Hollywood.

'Where'd you get your yellow boot strings, Bastion?'

I looked down at the yellow boot laces in my black leather jump boots. I knew enough already about life, green behind the ears as I was, to say little and listen a lot. Then people think you know more than you actually do, and they respect you that much more. It gives you an edge, especially in a hostile environment like Los Angeles. Chances of survival while struggling at street level are slim to none. Statistics happen every day on those lonely, filthy streets.

'I got these at *Retail Slut* just down the street.'

'*Slut* got anymore? I'm a Rude Boy too— just don't have the strings to prove it. You know how it is.'

Then it dawned on me. Stickman assumed that I was a Skinhead like him. My hair was pretty short, and in '89 that was unusual anywhere in America, but especially in 'Heavy Metal Land.'

'Careful of the White Supies,' he said. 'Not many around here, but a few. But I guess you know that.'

I said nothing. I nodded as if I knew what he was talking about. *White Supies. Hmmm*— got it! White supremacists.

'See many Blue Boys around?'

Stickman was either referring to cops, or to another color boot string I had to decipher.

'Not many,' I replied as I caught myself rubbing my hand even harder on my thigh, trying to get Stickman's infectious germs off me before I wiped my face or put my fingers in my mouth. I then got another whiff of his oral fetor. I nearly vomited.

'You alright? Maybe you're hungry. Let me get you a slice of that good old New York style pizza. I've got green.'

'No. I'm okay, Stickman. Thanks though.'

'No really. *Here.* Take this Hamilton and get yourself a burger.'[1]

'No really, Stickman. I'm alright. I've got money too.'

'You sure?' He lifted an eyebrow and gazed at me, trying to convince himself I was alright. Then he unrolled his pack of cigarettes from his tight white t-shirt sleeve.

'Wanna fag, dude? Sorry I didn't ask.' He knocked one out and lit up with a shiny silver Zippo he pulled out of his left pants pocket.

'No thanks,' I replied.

'I can get you weed if you want it. *The kindest.* I can get you anything you want. *Anything,* dude. Hey, what did the vampire say to the new guy in town?'

I shook my head and shrugged.

'I can get you any fang!'

That hit my funny-bone, but the conversation, even with the joke, was making me nervous.

---

[1] $10. USD. In Hollywood in the late 80s, a hearty char-broiled burger, a drink, and a load of fries were about $5.

'Ha! Think I could do stand-up, Bastion? No, really. I *can* get you anything. And when I say *anything*, I do mean *anything*.'

'I don't need any fang—I mean *thing*—but thanks anyway,' I said, now very nervous.

'Course, there'll be a price—' he added.

I went cold and stepped away from him.

'Oh! *Ha*! I didn't mean *that*, dude! *Damn*! I just meant, well, never mind. But I didn't mean *that*! Damn dude!'

Apparently my friendship meant something important to Stickman. I began to think that he didn't belong to a Skinhead gang at all, and that he had adopted the style as a way of personal expression in Tinseltown.

'Yeah. Blue Boys are really cool,' he said. 'Their anti-racism is the raddest thing I've ever seen. See, I'm from behind the 'Orange Curtain.' Supies rule down there! By the way, where you from, Bastion? I think I might detect a little Pensacola, Florida in there somewhere. Am I right?'

I was astounded. I had no idea that the city of my birth had its own dialect recognizable the world over.

'You're right alright,' I replied. 'Dang, Stickman. How'd you do that?'

'*Dang*? Ha-ha! Who says 'dang?''

I felt stupid.

'I've been livin' on these streets since I was thirteen, dude,' he added. 'I'm nineteen now. Lots— and I mean *lots* of Southerners skulk down these boulevards. I conversate a lot. With everybody. And after a while, you can pick up the subtle nuances. Yours is definitely 'Pensacola.' It's similar to, well, I was gonna say Mobile, Alabama, but that's not true. Pensacola has a definite sound of its own—the old dialect anyway, not this here new Redneck Riviera bumpkin bullshit. Nothin' else like old school P'cola talk, really. It's just classic—and seems to be a dying art. You've got a bit of it, but not much. What's funny, though, is that I didn't know there were Rude Boys in the Deep South. I figure there might be Supies, that area bein' the hotbed of 'Civil Wrongs' and all, but yellow-laces? You must be an old Punk. That right?'

Now Stickman was talking my language. 'Yeah. I'm into Punk,' I said, yielding the obvious. 'Have been since '79.'

'Yep. You're an original then. Explains the yellow.'

This whole thing about yellow boot strings was making little sense to me, and what made everything more disconcerting was I didn't know where this street waif, if you can call a nineteen-year-old a *waif,* was heading with his pigeonholing story. Maybe he was headed nowhere.

'So, you a Punk, or a Skin? Or what?' Stickman asked me, apparently not having really heard my confession. I wanted to tie up loose ends with this guy, so to speak. I had other things to do and see before sunset, when I planned to take a leisurely stroll down Sunset.

'I'd say a Punk,' I replied, giving him room for his inattention. 'Though I've studied the whole Skinhead movement pretty close. Listen, *ah—*'

'Pretty intricate, ain't it,' Stickman replied with a smile way too wide for his skinny face. 'I love how it all started. Jamaican metalworkers in London shavin' their heads so the tiny pieces of metal wouldn't get caught next to their scalp and cut in and make sores. Then the suspenders instead of belt buckles that get in the way of machine tables. Loose pants to keep cool around all that hot machinery. Doc Marten boots because they're the best for the feet, especially if you have to stand on them for 8 to 10 hours at the time. And then the frustration-releasin' Ska music, the forerunner of Reggae. You like *Madness,* dude?'

'*Our house!*' I sang off-tune, '*is a very, very, very fine house!*'

'No! *Damn!*' Stickman said. 'That's that damn Hippie band. What's their fuckin' name?'

I didn't know. I had only heard the song once or twice.

'Naw, dude! The *Madness* song goes like this: *Our house! In the mid-dle of the street!* You know. *That* one. Remember it now?' Both his eyebrows shot up.

'Oh yeah. That one.' Though music was (and still is) a favorite topic of mine, I was feeling tired and a little bored with the conversation. All in all, though, this kid was a nice guy, if not altogether trustworthy. I had already met some real doozies in Hollywood. Take my first landlord, for instance, who lived in his own basement with a woman he routinely beat up in front of her four-year-old girl and his Gay lover who started out as his pizza delivery boy. Or what about the Mexican who chased the Black man down Santa Monica Blvd. with a pigsticker the size of a small machete, hiding behind garbage cans and parked cars as he stalked. Who needs Hell after all, eh?

Not long before the present dialogue with my new S&M chicken friend, I went into the *Burger King* on Hollywood, not far from the Chinese Theatre, and was staggered and angered by the loudmouthed night manager telling the woman ahead of me that she could *not* have it her way,[1] that she would have it *his* way, or not at all. When she protested, he told her to shut up and order or get out of his restaurant. She ordered nonetheless, and when I stepped up to the register, he must have seen the anger in my eyes, because he repeated his threat to me. I took my bag of ten hamburgers, sneered at him, and never darkened his door again. As I passed the Chinese Theatre, I saw a homeless man I recognized as a local. I walked over and offered him a burger. He screamed at me that he should kill me for my obsequious derangement and that my sycophanticatory fawning over all astute deliriums should order me, internally, to take my hamburgers back to whatever insidiatory slum-lord had instigated me to relay gangrenous poisons unto him for his deleterious and possibly even ruinous death by masticatorial chewinisation. Instead of running away crying for help, I sat down (obviously with somebody else's bravery) next to the delirious fellow, and we became fast friends in a matter of five minutes. After a fashion, he pulled a dirty piece of paper out of his pocket and, with a blue ink pen that magically appeared between his fingers, he drew a picture of a surfboard shooting over a giant half-filled drug syringe, and explained that he knew I loved surfing and the water, and that I had deep dreams unfulfilled in that area. The guy was dead on. He then ate two of my burgers and excused himself, as he needed to congregate with other souls willing to involve themselves in placatory infractions concerning social environmentation, implementing their coagulatory disorientations to the best of their permeatorial designations.

That's Hollywood for you. It's not (and never has been) what they put on television or the silver screen. Not by a long shot.

♪

Back to Stickman.

'So, dude. *Bastion*. *Retail Slut* got more yellow strings?'
'I think I bought their last pair.'

---

[1] The tagline for Burger King was once *Have It Your Way*.

'That sucks. I've looked all over the city for yellow strings.
I even went to *Poseur*.'

'Poseurs?' I heard myself ask, immediately sorry I had.

'*Yeah*. The Punk outfit. You haven't been in yet?'

'No.'

'Come on then. Let's go. They're cool. You set okay? I can
leaf you a few 'til payday if you need it. Can I have your
strings? I'll buy you some white ones and then we'll dye them
yellow. Okay? I know where we can snake some yellow dye.'

'Snake?'

'Steal, dude. *Snatch. Rip off*.'

'Why don't you do that yourself?'

'Do what?'

'Buy white strings and dye them yellow.'

'Because you live in a house and I don't,' he replied in a
meek tone. It must have been obvious that I wasn't on the
street, and this made me feel naked.

'I don't think I feel like goin' to a Punk clothing and
accessory store right now, Stickman. I'm tired. I work on my
feet eight hours a day, five days a week. Or, to be more
accurate, 39 hours a week?'

'Fuckin' corporate bastards. So scared you'll work a few
minutes overtime. Anyway, your choice, dude. Sure do like
them strings. Well, I gotta get goin'. Workin' all night. I'm set
up *good* tonight, dude. Lawyer convention in Century City.'
He lolled his tongue out like some kind of thirsty desert
reptile. I thought about this, and then realized he *was* a
thirsty desert reptile. And I would be, too, and in no time at
all if I didn't do something quick to change my street-level
environment and the animals that inhabited it.

6

L.A. Woman

She calls me again, my lover, my desolation. She loves me, adores me. I need to be near her, to be in her. They call my name and rip me, thinking they do good. How I love them. How I love them all. I am a sinner, and the most undeserving for the Host. Yet my love for him is great; self-defiled I stand of late and cry to him in selfish stance. If need be, let him use the lance that pierced his own body and soul, that all demons may lose control over my body and my mind. I long to be gentle and kind. I need his love, I need his care, I need to know that he is near. For this great city is a fire that burns each day with renewed ire. A hellish pit of vile decay that lets no one stand in its way. Angel on a bed of silk and milky things. Angel in my arms. She calls me again. My lover. My desolation. I see you all of the time fall. The lonely electricity of the city, a gnawing quiet amidst millions of reverberations. Hollywood darkness is the darkest darkness. Hollywood. A faithless place. Hopelessness on each lost face. A painful hunger to survive the hate in every eye. Nothing will change, but for the worse because we carry on the curse from our fathers to our sons—disobeying, ever running.

Forget about a plan for peace; nothing shall ever give release. Nothing could now give us a chance: we love our disobedience. The rest we like to say is 'free' is bitter fruit of anarchy. Hollywood. Decadent. A ghost of its former glory. Here, seekers seek, dreamers dream, and aimless youth while their lives away in search of the perfect high. Hollywood steams at night. Every eye watches, waiting for what may happen— that certain thing that will change one life, or many. That certain thing, that magical thing, never manifests. Only its shadow is felt, towering above the Chinese Theatre. Heart to heart, eye to eye, my soul tortured each time they cry. We are the evil. We are the unholy. We are the damned. Is there hope for tortured souls? We hate this world. We fight its hold. Yet all around, in all our towns, everywhere we go we are bought and sold like stupid beasts on Rodeo Drive. Be warned brother, sister. Lust for money takes your life. City of masks, desolate and so lost, so foreign—not America as most see America—as most prefer to see America—as most would like America to be—America the

beautiful, America the free—well, taste this place and its agony. You need to be here. Alone. At night. In Hell. Sometimes I can hardly breathe. I am trapped, and I know it. I have loved her in this midnight as she lay sleeping, longing for a pretty day. She lay breathing desert night with visions of a little girl truly loved and given hope. People have lived in Los Angeles all their lives yet have never seen the houses of the dead. Should I cough up blood and die, would you wipe it from my eyes? Little whores. They are our sisters. Stand in Hollywood on the brink of Hell's divorce from Love. I love you. Do you love me? Who really loves the secrets of the darkened streets at night? Who really loves a life of never seeing light? If given other choices would you walk away from pride? Or would you stay and never pray and live in Sodom tonight? They take the streets at night behind the old drugstore, emerge at Cahuenga; how I love Hollywood whores. Don't look at me that way anymore. God, I love them. Like you do. I know how you feel. You tell me all the time. At dawn all the night is gone that holds my comforts, things remembered—things a child so loves to feel, to know, to see. Love them. Breathe the toxic air. Angels Lost.
quiet
cold
no eyes
no hands
can't try
lost hope
lost life
lost land
    Awake, my lover. Awake, my dear. Awake, my precious. Never fear. This wake is not for you, my precious. This wake is not for you. My walls bleed. Not my Hollywood walls, but the walls of my soul, because it seems that given all I have, I dream my time away in Hell. How I love you. You will die, you know. You will die some night when I'm asleep and shadows creep to my cold side and spit the truth 'She's dead. She died.' She says that love makes her feel bad. She says she cries sometimes all day. She says she prays so hard, so sad. They took you, sweet darling girl and hanged you on their wall. But the limelight was so bright no one saw you would fall. And when you fell you broke into ten trillion tiny parts, one of which works its way deeper, always, to my heart. Please forgive them all. Victims of the Fall. I am so tired. I war for you, you know. Are you watching me while I walk

away into death? Do you even see me? God, save from harm these lonely children no one sees in our dark cities, on our dark streets. Give me your eyes, give me your hands, give me your mind to understand. Give me your feet, keep me alarmed. Give me your arms to keep them warm. I am the light of each lost fire. I am the flame of each lost name and all desire. Do you have a heart that bleeds in sacrifice? The neighbor girl. The girl you went to school with. The girl you held, she cried on your shoulder. Remember? How do you see yourself? I see a queen. How do you see yourself? I see pristine beauty; a precious girl needing but one dream to come true. I have for you that dream. Do you remember me?

Of course your heart is sad and low. This place of darkness we all know.

7

Margie

Margie lived at the Regency when I moved in. *Funny*. I never knew where she worked, or even if she had a job. But she *had* to have a job. It was Hollywood. And she wasn't a prostitute like some of my other friends at the Regency. At least I don't think she was.

Margie was a super-petite Mexican girl from Chicago—a *pequeñita*. She never told me why she moved to Hollywood. The O'Neill boy, a drummer, who lived in the apartment next door to me—and two doors down opposite Margie—said he had dated her a year or so before I moved in. Close proximity to each other, I guess. She wanted to be with me, I could tell—but I didn't want to be with anybody. I loved her, though—felt close to her, but had no desire to be with her in any other way.

Margie told me she was a Christian, and I believed her, because one night she knocked on my door, and there she stood with an armload of warm Mexican wool blankets, mostly blue in color. She wanted me to go out on the Boulevard with her so we could give them to homeless people. We did. That hour is still one of my favorite memories of Hollywood.

Margie said she was suicidal—after I pulled it out of her like a wisdom tooth. She felt deeply ashamed by the fact. I think she stayed in bed for a whole day after that.

I have often thought of Margie through the decades, and this little sketch about her is a prayer for her. I'd like to see her again one day.

A Christian girl giving away free wool blankets on a freezing Hollywood night. Unbelievable, I know, but I was there to witness it.

8

Suzanne

The back parking lot of the Regency was eerily quiet to be a half block off Hollywood Blvd. and only a door or two north of the world-famous and tourist-infested Chinese Theatre.

'I see you're back in Hollywood, Bastion. Good to have you back.'

I was taking a bag of garbage out to the industrial-size dumpster at the same time Donald Luan was. I had never seen him away from his door frame or outside his apartment. It scared me. He looked strange. More imposing than he always had leaning in the dim hallway to chat softly with me as he smiled and nodded congenially. This afternoon the sun blazed so hot that his white hair shone with a particular brightness, almost otherworldly. In short, Don looked lean and mean to be a man of his age.

'How was working with Euseb Pappastephanou?'

'I never told you I was leaving, Don, much less what I was going to do after I left.'

'Are you surprised I know?' The familiar gentle tone was there in his voice.

'I guess not. No.'

'One day it'll all come together for you. I have some hot fried chicken breasts on the stove. Care to come in for a bite? Collards, too. With pepper vinegar. And cornbread. I was just about ready to sit down to supper.'

'Well— got any sweet tea?'

'Just made a fresh pitcher. I be honored if you ate with me. I've missed you, son. Come on in and catch me up.'

I felt funny about it at first, but then I felt a calm fall over me, and really, quite a bit of joy. 'I'd like that a lot, Don. It's great to see you again. Let me step down the hall and get some chips or something to go with supper. Some coke or something. What kind of coke do you like?'

'Now I can for *sure* tell you're from the Deep South. Got any Nu-Grape?'

'Sure do.'

'Bob Haggard give you the same room you had?'

'Sure did. It was empty.'

'Not surprised, son. Not surprised at all.'

♪

'I got a strange phone call the other day, Bastion. The voice on the other end said he was Arlo Costanada, and that he wants to meet you.'

I stopped eating my chicken breast. The meat hung in my mouth until it was tepid and either needed to be swallowed or spit out. I finished chewing it up. Then I sucked down my whole cherry cola in one gulp. I still couldn't talk.

'Oh, I thought you were a witch-finder. Sorry. I guess I have the wrong Bastion, or maybe Bastion left all of his anti-witch weapons back in Florida with that monk-priest Euseb. In either case, I apologize for broaching the subject. So, how 'bout them 'Noles?'

'I'm not too much into basketball.'

'Apparently not. Or football either, looks like. *Bastion.* You've just a few minutes ago told me that you came back to Los Angeles to go to war. So what gives? You chicken?' He laughed at his own accidental joke.

'More like a turkey,' I replied. 'Gobble, gobble, gobble.'

Don smiled. I could see God in his eyes. 'Here, let me tell you a story, Bastion. Maybe it'll lighten up the scene here for a few minutes.'

'Okay. I like stories. Good ones, anyway. Shoot.'

'Alright. Let's see here now. Once upon a time, in 1943, when this building, the Regency, was two years old and only rented out to young female starlets, Hollywood, as you know, was fairly ritzy—and muscle-controlled, of course. As if that still isn't the case. Anyway, there was a rule of the house here at the Regency, though, that you not only had to be single and female, but you couldn't have children. Now, there was this raven beauty who lived here. Her name was Margarite Sheehan—a gorgeous young actress by all accounts. Lauren Bacall's darker sister, some said. You get the picture. Sort of a precursor to Elizabeth Taylor, maybe. Anyway, while Margarite lived here she met and fell madly in love with a budding but not yet successful film director. Well, Margarite soon enough got herself *in the family way,* as it were, with this director. She had no money to move again, since she hadn't landed a substantial part yet and her work as a waitress out here on the Boulevard paid just enough for her to get her rent together by the end of each month. What would she do, and how would she keep the secret of her baby from her landlord who, like Bob Haggard, lived here on-site?

Margarite decided, though, that she would stay on here at the Regency. To accomplish this was an actor's greatest role, seemingly, and she was up for the challenge. With help from a few friends who lived here, and no thanks to the vanishing father of the child, who, by the way, never made it in 'the Biz,' Margarite managed to keep her weight down enough to make it seem like she had only put on a few pounds. Remember, back then female stars were a little heftier than they like to be today. If today's rule were in place back then, Margarite would seem oddly out of shape for an actor. But as it stands, she just became, well, *full*. In other words, she became even more desirable for films than she had been *before* her pregnancy. Ironically, her new condition kept her from auditioning, but her landlord believed she had just fallen on hard times, and taking her stunning beauty into account, allowed her to stay on here in the building even though she wasn't a 'working actress.' She paid her rent, and that's all he really cared about. Fortunately for Margarite, Hal Johnson wasn't the meddlesome type. Anyway, the big day finally came, and it was a bouncing baby boy she named Jack, after her grandfather who had been the only member of her family proud to see her try her fortune on the mean streets of Hollywood. But what would she do now? She had to begin auditioning again, and also keep her night job at the cafe. *A babysitter*. It was the only way. But who in Hollywood could babysit for her? She scraped money together and placed an advertisement in the Sunday paper. She set it up so the job applicants could meet her during her supper break at work. She would play them off as friends who had come to visit her. She got three responses the first day, three the next, two the next, and one more as that issue of the newspaper became blankets for hobos. The first three people to apply for the job were duds; all unsuccessful starlets with varied unattractive baggage from prowling ex-boyfriends to ideas of moving back home to Kansas, or Florida, or wherever else they had taken a train from. The next day, a man in his early 40s met her. He talked too much about how much he loved children—especially little girls. After he left, a Mexican migrant worker and his wife came, but revealed during conversation that they already had five children, the youngest three no older than five years. Just as they left, a young girl came in, nicely dressed and happy. Margarite liked her immediately. The second to last day, an elderly but able woman came in, but she was obviously mentally ill, as she grunted like a pig, barked like a dog, or bleated like a sheep every time Margarite mentioned baby Jack. The day after that, the well-dressed happy girl came back to see if Margarite had found someone. She was hired, and the two became fast friends almost overnight. The girl's name was Suzanne. *Alright.* So Margarite hires Suzanne to babysit for her, but what she doesn't know—what Suzanne has not told her—is that the young girl lives alone in a mansion in the hills not far from here, up around Argyle. Her parents, both of them independently wealthy socialites, have been missing for six months, and Suzanne has never reported it to the authorities. No one today has been able to find the exact house, it's been so many years. This story has turned into almost a local legend. Well, the first night comes that Suzanne is supposed to babysit, and since it's already been difficult to keep Jack from being heard crying, arrangements are made for Suzanne to keep him at her own house, which has been imaginarily peopled for Margarite's benefit with a mother and father and two older sisters. For some reason Margarite doesn't check into the matter. She trusts Suzanne, likes her very much, and believes her every word. And, of course, she's desperate. Apparently Suzanne seemed completely credible. Now, story has it that the little girl knew the combination to her parents' wall safe, and that inside it was enough money and jewels to comfortably retire on. So she was set for food, clothes, taxis, lights, fuel for the fireplaces; everything she could ever need. So why babysit? The first night arrives and Margarite hires a taxi to drop Jack off at the house. Suzanne greets them at the head of the circular drive and assures the baby's mother that he'll be in the safest possible hands. Margarite is pleased with how she feels about the responsible young girl, and is deeply impressed by the mansion in which she lives. She works six nights a week, and so needs Suzanne each night. I know. It's funny. The story slips on Margarite not asking about school, or to meet her parents or her sisters. But this happened over 40 years ago, and legend traditionally leaves out lots of detail. Anyway, the babysitting went on for several months, no questions asked, no inquiries made, everybody happy. Jack grew quick and strong. In the daytime when Margarite went to auditions, friends here at the Regency kept him— including the manager Hal Johnson who found out about Jack but was too fond of Margarite at that point to even care. Six nights a week Suzanne kept Jack until two in the

morning, and then had a taxi bring them back here to
Margarite. Anyway, one night the taxi arrived with only Jack
in it, packed into a wicker basket jammed securely behind
the front seat on the floorboard. And to make things
stranger, the taxi this night was a Rolls Royce. Margarite
asked the driver about Suzanne, and when he didn't know,
but said that a strange man in a long cowboy oil-coat had
placed Jack there and paid an extraordinary amount of
money to deliver him, Margarite had him drive her and Jack
to the mansion. Leaving the baby in the temporary care of
the kindly and already well-compensated driver, she
approached the mansion. Its door was ajar, and, as far as she
could see, everything seemed to be in perfect order.
Margarite was hesitant, as you can imagine. She lit a candle
that sat on a foyer table. Then, scared but brave, she explored
each room, both downstairs and upstairs, the eerie attic, and
the terrifying cellar. *Nobody.* Not even sleeping servants, as
she fully expected, thinking maybe the parents were out. But
where was Suzanne and her sisters? One day, about a week
later, in early afternoon, Margarite went back to the big
house to look for Suzanne, but again, there was no one at
home. The actress was bumfuzzled. Where could the girl be?
In short order, Suzanne was forgotten in the hustle and
bustle of Hollywood life. Jack grew older, and Margarite
suddenly hit it really big and moved out of this building into
her own mansion. But wait. There's more. The most
important part. One day as Margarite was teaching Jack how
to walk, she decided to let him toddle with her up North
Orange out here to Franklin. When she got him to the
corner, she saw Suzanne! The girl beckoned to Margarite,
and smiled like the Cheshire Cat.'
   Don stopped, leaned back in his chair, and closed his
eyes.
   'You're finished?'
   'Yep.' His mouth twitched with a barely hidden glee.
   'You have *got* to be kidding me!'
   'Got *that* right! *Ha-ha!*'
   'Wait a minute! You—you made that story up?'
   'Sure did. Off-the-cuff, too.'
   'Just now? You made that cliffhanger up right here and
now?'
   Don opened his eyes. He chuckled.
   'No way! And I thought *I* was a storyteller! I'll never write
another sentence again!'

'You *are* a storyteller, Bastion. You just need a few more decades of practice is all. You'll get there. *Relax.* You've got a big day tomorrow, young man. Get some rest. I hear Costanada can smell insincerity faster than sharks sense blood.'

I left Don's apartment that night feeling like I had been in the presence of Humphrey Bogart or Orson Welles or Gregory Peck or some other luminous star of the silver screen. Truth is, Donald Luan out-shined them all.

9

Costanada

Arlo Costanada was almost exactly as I had imagined him.
Friendly, jovial, handsome, charismatic, and super smart.
His dark eyes snapped with intelligence. His voice, tinged
slightly with a Latino feel because of his Peruvian
background, was commanding yet affable. He was dressed
sharp in a pair of pleated khaki slacks, a lime Panama shirt,
chocolate brown penny loafers complete with the shiny
coppers, and white crew socks. His coal black hair was
longish, thick, and brushed back in a classic easygoing,
almost effortless style.

'I understand, Bastion, that you want to know more about
our lineage—the *brujos* and *brujas* with whom I associate.'
The black cougar at his side looked at me aggressively. 'This
is Goliath. He's also a sorcerer, but he made a drastic mistake
and succeeded in getting himself trapped as a feline, where
he has to remain until his last dance for freedom—his last
battle. He doesn't mind me telling you about it. Do you
Goliath?' The cougar nudged Costanada's thigh with his
nose. 'Would you like to hear exactly what happened to
Goliath?'

'Mr. Costanada' I was as nervous as a rooster under a tree
full of hawks. I fought the urge to get right to the point.
That's my style. Cut to the chase. No beating around the
bush. Get right down to brass tacks.

'*Please*. Call me Arlo.'

'Okay. *Arlo*. Sure, tell me Goliath's story. I like stories.'

Even though it was Hollywood, no wild animals are
allowed to be kept as pets in California. This means all non-
domestic canines and felines, which include panthers. So
how had Costanada been able to walk into the restaurant
with Goliath? I didn't ask, and nobody, not even our waitress
Gilda, seemed to mind, or even be interested.

'Goliath was born a while back. Let's just say before *I* was
even alive.'

The giant animal hopped up beside me in the booth, then
rested his chin on my shoulder, growling. I was horrified.
New freaky experience, I told myself. *This is Hollywood,
right? What else should I expect?* Costanada grinned and
continued with his story.

The Teachings of Don Luan

'Goliath began his life as a hardworking Tongva Indian named *Taamit* in his language, which means 'Sun.' Taamit picked fruit for a living, mostly oranges and peaches here in the Los Angeles Basin, since they are year-round crops.'

'Wait. Arlo, how do you know Goliath's story? Last time I checked, panthers don't talk.' The cougar pulled his head back and stared at me as if not believing I had actually interrupted the story. A cold chill shot up and down my spine. Satisfied that he had terrified me, he lay his chin down on my shoulder again and shut his frightening greyish-green eyes.

'Goliath wrote it all down before he transformed. I have the signed document.'

I felt like an idiot.

'You feel like an idiot, don't you, Bastion. Well, trust me, I did too after I called the Los Angeles Zoo and reported an escaped black mountain lion. I felt even stupider when they sent a team of zoologists out to investigate and I couldn't produce a panther for them because Goliath here, despite his appearance, is not an animal. He knew they were coming to drug and take him somewhere he didn't want to be, so he conveniently disappeared. Truthfully, I don't know anybody who would enjoy that scenario. So, anyway, to get on with the story, one day our Tongva friend here met two finely dressed gentlemen; Mr. James Avelar and Mr. Alonso Grey. The men were unusually kind to him, because all he ever usually got from people of European extract were harsh condescending stares and snappy work orders. His ethnic background and lack of education offered him only the disadvantage of working as essentially a slave in his own ancestral homeland. But his meeting Grey and Avelar changed everything, because these two men had reinvented the secret to life, and had then founded the sorcery lineage of which I am now the last leader called to disseminate the mysteries we have kept close for generations, which include the weird, druidic, creepy Old Shamans as well as, of course, us New Shamans fostered by Grey and Avelar.'

'Of course,' I replied, trying hard not to sound mocking. This whole thing was a prime load of *caca*, and I believe Costanada saw the mockery in my eyes. He hesitated, but then seeming to disregard what he noticed, he continued with Goliath's story.

Taamit became an educated gentleman and an entrepreneur under the tutelage of Grey and Avelar, who thought it would be funny for him to take the name *Goliath* since it was obvious to them, and obvious to many people today, that the giant Goliath was only doing his job by protecting his Philistine people from the warmongering Hebrews. Right?'

I felt suddenly furious. I had to interrupt. 'That sounds pretty antisemitic to me, Arlo. Are you some kind of backwater Jew-hater?'

Costanada shrugged and grinned. 'Anyway, not many years later Goliath owned his *own* orange groves and peach orchards. He was good to his workers, gave them excellent pay and benefits for their valuable services, and treated them and their family members with kindness. He remained close to his two teachers, and before too much time had passed there came a number of others—both men and women—to join the three in their unique pursuit of freedom. Well, one day Goliath came across a locked chest owned by Avelar. His curiosity got the best of him, so he picked the lock and opened the coffer. Inside, among other books and bound papers, was an old Spanish grimoire that dated back to the 16th Century. Inside it Goliath found, written in the *Español* he could now fluently read, speak, and write, certain methods by which a sorcerer could transform himself into anything else, animal or vegetable or mineral, and then come back into human form when the time was desired to do so. In essence, the soul could migrate into another body while at the same time forcing the present occupant to pass away from it. In the case of an animal, its spirit would die but its body would be reanimated by the sorcerer before it no longer functioned. In the case of another human, well, if they weren't in a state of awareness, it was all fair game and he or she had to find another body or learn to live in the spirit world. Sounds like cold-blooded murder, I know—and it really is, but so what? All's fair in love and war, right?'

'Sure thing, Arlo. If you're into full-blown relative thinking—which I'm not.'

Goliath opened his eyes and stared straight into my soul like a demon starving for something human.

Arlo took a drink of water and cleared his throat. 'But what did the old book say about the *former* body of the sorcerer—his human form? Well, a concoction was prescribed—one that would be made of several rare but attainable herbs that commonly grow in the L.A. Basin. Pure sorcery in action—the mastery of potency. So ol' Goliath here wrote down everything about his life up to the moment, signed it, followed the book's concoction recipe to a fault, made the drug, ingested it, left his body lying on his bed, and went in search of the animal he most admired—the 'Florida cougar,' and a black one at that. Needless to say, he found his prey and quickly displaced the spirit of the regal animal. He knew that both of his teachers would have strongly disapproved, because this despicable act was more in line with those of the slavery-minded Old Shamans, not the freedom-minded New Shamans. Yet knowing that he delved into extremely dangerous territory, and having understood from the grimoire that there was a good chance that any *brujo* who set out to practice this particular feat could find himself trapped in the animal's body, he persisted almost as if he had been possessed.'

I nodded. Goliath had indeed been possessed. The big cat lifted his head and looked at me again. I got the uncanny sense that he could read my thoughts, and that he didn't like them very much at all.

Costanada paused and took a huge bite of his burger. He closed his eyes with pleasure. 'I always love the food here, Bastion. Dig in! So anyway, becoming trapped had happened before, the treatise stated, with only half a chance of being able to come back to the dormant human body. And in some cases when the sorcerer was able to return to his original abode, that body was already dead for some unknown reason, so he had to scramble to find yet another body, stone, tree, or whatever to inhabit before his spirit was lost in darkness. To make matters even worse, only certain plants would accept the spirits of sorcerers. Most, however, rejected them outright. But, as we can plainly see, Goliath wasn't able to escape the body of the cougar, so here he is, awaiting his day of freedom when he and the rest of us burn with 'the flame from within,' as is taught, and leave together for eternal life as our reward for the impeccability we have fostered and lived.

'Pelagian.'

'Say what?'

I backpedaled. 'Oh, nothing Arlo. Just clearing my throat. *Pelag*!'

He stared at me for a few seconds, and then beamed. 'Alright then! So, there's the story of your new friend there. How'd I do, Goliath?'

The cougar turned from me to Costanada and put both his paws on the table. Then he sniffed our plates of food, obviously hungry. Costanada gave the big cat half of his huge cheeseburger and a handful of fries. I looked around to see if anybody was watching. No one in the establishment seemed to notice. I felt like I was in the *Twilight Zone*. I could even hear the freaky music of the show playing in my head. *Doo-doo-doo-doo—Doo-doo-doo-doo*

'Bastion, join us. I can see that your spirit configuration is perfect for what we do. Ask for whatever you want. Wealth, honor, Hollywood fame. You name it. All yours for the taking. Everything is relative. You need to be evolved to see that there is no right and wrong—that it's all about your personal freedom. There is no stigma of so-called 'Original Sin'—no false guilt, no blind dependence on man-made law, and certainly no Sacrificial Lamb. Join us and you will find freedom. You can become the shape of your fantasies, fly to distant and even unknown places, control your eternal destiny, and assist with the destinies of others. True wisdom will be yours. Sound good?'

'Good story, Arlo,' I replied, 'but I only eat from the Tree of Life, and I won't play games here. You need to know what I have in mind. After all, you called Don Luan to say *you* wanted to meet *me*, remember?'

Costanada leaned back in the red leather diner booth. 'Alright, Bastion. Yes, I did seek you out because I could sense your presence here in Los Angeles and, true enough, would like to know what you're all about. So what do you have in mind? A film, maybe? Photographs? Both of those, by the way, are out. Nothin' doin'. We don't let people see what we look like. So, unless you are a straight journalist or a radio personality, or a fiction writer with a new hook that hasn't been done before—or maybe just a curious student who wants to know more about the magical worlds we have discovered and continue to discover, then you can finish lunch, on me, but that'll be about it.'

'I'm a witch-finder. One of the many who are declaring war on Los Angeles.'

Costanada pulled his chin in and gazed at me incredulously. Then he began to laugh—a gleeful, unaffected laugh that was the perfect mixture of a chuckle and a guffaw. A good, solid belly laugh. 'You mean, like the Witch-Finder General? Get outta here! Really?'

'Something like that, except I'm not Puritan and I don't torture people or burn them at the stake.'

'No? Then what do you do when you corner your quarry?'

'I wait.'

'For what? Just move in for the kill, man. Infinity has very little patience with wishy-washy warriors.'

Wow. Costanada really took his stuff seriously. Yet somehow he frowned on the freaky Old Shamans and their black magic. I didn't get it. 'Infinity, Arlo, as you understand it anyway, is a figment of your imagination. Infinity—eternity—is an absence of time measurement. That's all. It doesn't have a personality, and neither can it be patient or impatient. It's a creature, like every other creature made by God. It's like when you hear people saying they thank the Universe for this and that. You might as well thank the oak tree outside for whatever it is you're thankful for. Or the squirrel who hops around in its branches.'

'Well, if nothing else, I see that you are quite educated to be, how old? Eighteen? Twenty? Excellent background. I'm impressed.'

'Mid-twenties, and yes, though I am socially retarded most of the time, I have an ability with philosophical concepts—which most of the time I can't put into words to save my silly life. In fact, I'm so surprised that I'm able to talk with you that I feel like I'm somebody else doing the talking for me.'

'Right. Gotcha. Aaron and Moses as two separate parts of you. Aaron talks, Moses acts. I know the feeling. Same thing used to happen to me, and still does sometimes when I'm in the presence of someone who is publicly lauded as being important. I met Liza Minnelli the other day at a book signing and thought I was going to come unhinged I was so excited. Come to think of it, I guess I may seem to be one of those sorts to you.'

'Well, you've written quite a number of best-sellers that have been translated into every language of the world, so, yeah, you could say that.'

'Read any of them, have you?'

'How did you know I was looking for you, Arlo? Wait, I'll answer that myself. You're a witch. You use the power of God for your own purposes, even though you give God *no* credit for that power.'

'I don't? How so? I give all credit to the Eagle.'

'In no writing previous to yours, and yours alone, is there mention of self-garnered impeccability or perfection which leads us to a force called the Eagle. Jesus says that he—the Living Word—is the Way, the Truth, and the Life, and that no one comes to God except through him.'

'Who is this Jesus? Never heard of him. This is Los Angeles after all.' The look in Costanada's eyes was asking me if I got his joke.

'You talk about a lot of really cool things, Arlo. You even talk about love being the most powerful force in the universe. Why leave Jesus—the very source of love—out of the equation?'

'I claim the Fifth.'

'Your prerogative, I guess. Next question. Would you mind if I take the Bible scripture literally which mandates that I suffer not a witch to live?'

'I think I'd probably mind, yes. Would you mind if I take the Mexican mandate seriously which commands that no *gringo* be allowed to live—after, of course, he spends all of his money in Tijuana—or gets rolled for it, whichever comes first?'

'I wouldn't mind at all—if you can get past my guardian angels.'

Costanada, who had leaned forward during our semi-heated but still somewhat friendly exchange, seeming to enjoy the joust, leaned back again, his mouth open, his usually sharp eyes questioning and momentarily confused. He was perceptibly disarmed now, even astonished. Then I watched as a cloud of strengthening covered his features. He set his jaw, smiled, if weakly, and then turned to gaze out the large window next to us. We could clearly see the famous *Hollywood* sign from where we sat. 'Tell me what you see out there. Look over at that building directly across from us, on its roof just above the two windows below it, and tell me what is there. Do you see anything, Bastion?'

I closed my eyes, reopened them, narrowed them, and gazed.

'Perfect,' he said, interrupting me. 'You really are quite the warrior. Are you sure you work for Jesus? We could use a brilliant mind like yours, Bastion. I mean, even your name— pretty fucking powerful, man. *Bastion*.'

I had to bite my lower lip almost in half to keep from swelling out and away from my vision with his evident attempt to disarm me with smooth words of flattery.

'So, Bastion, what do you see where I asked you to look? Anything?' His words were almost a taunt. There was little exuberance left in him now. My honesty and forthrightness had worn him away as quickly as a sandcastle in a rainstorm.

I turned again and looked. 'Nothing. There's nothing up there.'

'Exactly!' he replied with a loud slap on the tabletop. 'Good eye! Good eye!' Now he was making outright fun of me. He had been overwhelmed with a surprise defeat by the mere mention of my guardian angels. He believed in them or he would have shrugged it off as another religious fantasy. This man was a true-blue witch—of the ilk who know who Jesus is yet still plan to try and trounce him one day. There's hardly any person more evil than to believe tantamount to how Hitler and the other Nazis thought—to how many people have believed through the millennia. That they can somehow defeat God in battle, which is like a mosquito thinking it can fly into a solar flare and survive.

'Well, all I can say is give it the old college try, Bastion,' Costanada finally replied with a mocking smirk and a false air of defeat. 'We won't stop you, or even try to. Well, I *say* that, but, on second thought, some of the women might take umbrage. La Mora, maybe. Or Ensueña, possibly. Then there's the three sisters—the Three Witches, we call them. Oh yes, then there's also Mama Tilo. Matter of fact, you may not survive after all. *Ha*! Six indomitable streetwise *brujas* against one little Christian boy still green in our world? *Nope*. Just can't see it. And I wish I could say it was nice knowing you, but it hasn't been, or that I'll miss you when you're gone, but I won't. Not in the slightest. In fact, good riddance. Freedom trumps Jesus, Bastion. Remember that. He was just a servant anyway—and a failure of one at that who got his ass kicked pretty royally! Fuck slain lambs and all that bullshit. People get crushed by all kinds of forces designed by Infinity on their behalf, so that they can, if they only will, attain a place, a platform, from which they can then vault themselves into freedom and, ultimately, into love— which is the source of everything, as you have so kindly brought up. Jesus failed that love, his followers failed that love, and you will fail that love. You are weak not because of what you desire, Bastion, but because of the idiot you follow. Personal strength, not weakness, is the key to freedom, to love, to Infinity, to the Eagle. What, after all, does his

Sacrificial Lamb bloodshed accomplish for you—for anybody? It's spilled milk. Nothing more.'

I knew he was dead wrong. Desire gets a person nowhere, but *will* gets that same person anywhere he'd like to be, and with God's people, that's always a place of full and powerful servitude. It was hard hearing Costanada curse and slander God, but I prayed for the help to endure. 'Then, Arlo, you have missed the whole point of the plight of mankind and our way out. And, you're sounding a lot like that fool Nietzsche. I recommend a closer reading of the Bible, and maybe a little prayer now and again. You'd be surprised at what you can learn when God *himself* actually teaches you. You're full of words and systems and books, but where's your power?' I took a much-wanted bite of my chili cheeseburger. It was still delicious even at room temperature. Then I pushed a few yummy pepper-covered greasy french fries into my hungry maw. *Mmmmm.*

Costanada went white around the gills, all of his former composure—his personality brand of mysterious seer and teacher—lost as his spirit madly struggled for self-empowerment in the face of the calm power I demonstrated for him. 'Fuck Jesus! Go to hell, Moses! And take your fucking inconsistent theology with you!'

'*Guardian angels,* remember.'

Costanada became as pale as cucumber flesh at the mention of them this time. His eyes darted behind where I sat. It seemed to me that he watched somebody back there. Then he got up from the table with a jerk and, without another word to me, a gesture, or even a simple 'goodbye,' he (and his panther) left the restaurant packed full of chatting, laughing, driven people primarily working in 'the Biz' in some capacity or another—producers, directors, actors, gaffers, best boys, lighting technicians, writers, film editors, security guards, the works. And it was no wonder they had all gathered there for lunch. The food was absolutely superb. Thankful that I had been able to hold my cool, I turned casually and raised my hand to call Gilda for our bill. As I did so, I saw one of my guardians. He leaned up against the back of a booth filled with beautiful, chatting young starlets, an easygoing look on his face. He exuded the same sort of power I had always experienced with my angels, when I knew they were there—when I had been allowed by God to see them. The feeling from them was, and still is, that nothing, no matter how prevailing in all of the cosmos, could get through just one of them should it try, be that enemy a single entity or an entire interstellar army. Nothing is able to accomplish its goal of my harm, or my death, as long as my guardians are dispatched to guard my life. And even in my death, they will be there to lift me up to the throne of my God and into his eternal habitations.

Yeah, you could say I was ready, whether I had known it before or not, to go to war against Arlo Costanada and whatever, or whomever, he had to offer in defense of his pseudo-intellectual sham system of belief. It was pretty evident that his wit and wisdom had failed him miserably over that cheeseburger and fries. Could he have killed me with his crystal daggers? If my angels hadn't been there to protect me, sure thing. I'd be a gonner. But they had, and that had changed the whole enchilada. *So, bring on the tacos*, I said to myself. *I've got plenty of hot sauce.*

I can be a real dork sometimes.

10

Marbella

She glowed like some kind of phosphorescent creature that cool desert night as she traipsed down the almost-two-dimensional Hollywood Boulevard, slow and measured, like the matron of a large country manor, or even a queen. I had heard of women like her from voices filled with horror and wonder. 'They're not everywhere, but once you see one, you'll never forget her as long as you live.'

But I had to do more than see one. I had to *talk* to one. If she would talk. If she knew where she was. If she knew she was alive.

The kinds of things that haunted me day and night in Hollywood? Mauve velvet curtains, brass pipe organs, 'monkey coffins', 78 rpm records, exotic *objets d'art*, pastel ostrich feathers, tuxedos in steamer trunks, wood molding, original S. Charles Lee ticket booths, flashbulb wool, Murphy beds, over-size magnifying glasses atop yellowed newspaper clippings, stiff black scrapbook pages, midnight swimming pools, pungent funeral flowers, clematis, old theater seats that creak *before* you sit in them, the pink 'cigarette burn' in the corner of a cinema screen, ill-advised taxidermy, cigarillo-smoking projectionists in mustard-stained tank-tops, pulp magazines, ridiculously slow ceiling fans, the back of a starlet's hand seemingly glued to her forehead—

As I came out of the Chinese Theatre after seeing a banal film, I saw her. I ran. I would catch her, but then what? What then? I didn't think further than that. I passed her, and slowed. Fifteen feet from her I turned, trying to be nonchalant, trying not to let her know that it was only me and her in my tiny world, nothing else, and that my heart burned to know. I had to know.

'I—'

She took a few more steps toward me in her unearthly gait as her faded blue feather boa fluttered in the breeze of a passing 'pirate cab' and her discolored teal silk evening gown shimmered in the ephemeral Hollywood breeze.

'You?' she replied, her puckered cigarette lips smiling, crow's-feet clawing at her sad, sad eyes.

'I want to know,' I said, breathless. 'How—how long. How long—'

'How long have I been living in Hollywood? Is that what you want to know, doll?'

I was suddenly frightened. My mind raced to the film *Sunset Boulevard*. I backed away from her and nearly disappeared into the shadows of a side street. But then I came back to my senses.

'Yeah— yes,' I replied. 'Yes ma'am.'

'Oh, a *Southern* boy!'

'Yes ma'am. Northwest Florida.'

'Oh my word! Why, I'm from Pensacola!'

Her accent wasn't Pensacolian in the least bit, but a pitch-perfect Transatlantic.

'Ma'am— now please don't think I'm lying to you, but I was born and raised in Pensacola.'

'Well, I have a way of telling whether you're lying to me or not, doll. What part of P'cola?'

I saw what she meant. 'Ferry Pass,' I replied.

'Ferry Pass. *Sure*! Out by the river. See? You're not a liar. A bit of a *lair*, maybe, but not a liar. Well, I was raised in Downtown Pensacola. On Sedona Square.'

'Pardon me, m'am, but there is no Sedona Square in Pensacola.'

She smiled. 'What square is it then?'

'Seville.'

'Yes, you are from Pensacola to be sure. But to answer that burning question of yours— say, doll? Would you like to have a drink with me at the *Carousel*?'

'Yes ma'am, and I'm buying.'

'Such a gentleman!'

♪

'I came to Hollywood in 19 and 43.' Marbella Hutchins fixed a Pall Mall into her shiny black 'opera length' cigarette holder. 'Forty-five years ago, give or take. Got a light, doll?'

'Yes ma'am,' I said as I fished around in my loose pants pocket for the cheapo lighter I always carried for no reason at all. 'May I be honest about something, Miss Hutchins?'

'You sure can, sweetheart.' She blew smoke in my face. Classy way to commit suicide—and murder. 'Honesty's all I got left. All I've had for lots of years now, come to think of it.'

'People think— people believe, *ah*, that women like you are, you know—'

The Teachings of Don Luan

'What? *Crazy*? Oh, I know that! Why do you think I'm
sitting with you right now, doll? You're the only person to
talk to me in close to a year, and the last time it was just a
hobo wanting a fag. I say something sometimes to a person I
know lives around here, not a tourist or anything like that,
and still all I get is a scared look in their eyes like 'Oh god!
That insane old broad just spoke to me!"
I felt like I wanted to cry. I went ahead and did just that.
Marbella handed me a bar napkin. It caught three teardrops
before it tore apart. She asked the barkeep Randy for a stack
of napkins, then handed me six more before I could fully
collect myself.
'You really care about people, don't you, doll?'
'More than anything, Marbella. I guess it's what I do best.
Then I go and write it all down.'
'Oh! A writer! I should have guessed—'
'Where did you first live here in Hollywood, Miss
Hutchins?'
'My first place was in the Regency, just a few buildings
north of the Chinese Theatre, on North Orange Drive.
Something wrong?'
'No,' I replied, realizing that my facial expression had
spoken out of turn. 'It's just that I live there is all. The
Regency. Which room was yours?'
'Second floor, second room on the left, as I remember.'
'That's *my* apartment!'
'Well what a coincidink!'
'There's talk of tearing the old place down. Least that's
what I hear.'
'I didn't need to know that, doll. That's not good news at
all. You know Marilyn and Bogie both lived there at different
times, don't you?'
'I heard that, yeah. Pretty thrilling. I've wondered if
maybe they lived in my apartment.'
'You keep saying *apartment*. Those are *rooms*, not
apartments, sweetheart.'
'I have, well— you know, a stove, refrigerator—'
'Oh. Well there was nothing like that in there when I lived
there. A Hollywood starlet had to eat at cheap diners and
hole-in-the-wall restaurants back then. Well, most of us.
Unless we involved ourselves in regular couch sessions, if
you know what I mean. Then the grill cheese magically
turned into a steak, the fried pie into *pie à la mode*, the

water into wine—or was it whisky. Fuzzy memory, been so long.'

'I see.'

'Do you? Maybe you do. You're a writer after all. Well, I can't imagine trying to cook in such a small place anyways. Not and have room for my dressing table and all my clothes. Do they still have those Murphy beds that fold down out of the closet?'

I nodded 'yes' and stirred my Shirley Temple. What should I ask Marbella next? I wanted to know it all, but how could I learn over a half-century of knowledge about a lady's life in an hour? Two hours? Three hours? Heck, even three weeks!

'You want to know how I've lived in Hollywood all these years? How I've survived?'

'Well, Miss Hutchins,' I replied sheepishly, sure that I had never heard of her or seen her in any film. 'Yes, I would like to know how you have survived. But I don't think it's any of my business, really.'

'I've just made it your business, haven't I? Listen, doll. I don't say anything I don't want to say. I never have, I never will. So here's the story. I am a wealthy heiress. That means I'm a princess of sorts. An old, worn-out princess that everybody thinks is crazy, but a princess nonetheless. Every year that flies by, though, less and less people pay attention to me. It used to hurt something awful, to be ignored. See, I was quite the actress in my day, though I never had more than bit parts even at the height of my career. But then parts quit coming along at all. I couldn't keep an agent. They all said I was 'over-the-hill.' *Lord*! I was only thirty-two! I could have gone back to Pensacola, but why? My mother and father were dead, I had no siblings, and what few relatives I had left wanted my inheritance. My father, a wise man when it came to money, sold all of his stock right before the Crash of '29, and then, just before the War, he and my mother were killed in an automobile accident. Everything they had saved went to me. I had a dream. I wanted to be a movie star. I came, I saw, and I *sort* of conquered. At any rate, I decided to stay here in Hollywood after my short-lived career began to decline. I had always lived cheap, preparing for the very real likelihood that I would never become a star. I never did, of course. You ever heard of 'The Great Marbella Hutchins?' My last job as an actor was in 1950.'

'But— but that's been almost forty years ago, Miss Hutchins!'

Marbella looked down at her Tom Collins and swirled the melting ice. 'Yes it has, hasn't it. Another drink for you, doll?'

'No ma'am. Thank you, though. Why— why do you— still dress as if you were attending a Hollywood soirée?'

She scowled. 'And why shouldn't I?' Then she smiled big and happy to let me know she had only pretended to be angry with me.

I felt truly embarrassed. I shouldn't have asked that question. 'I'm sorry,' I said. 'I dress how I feel. Why shouldn't you?'

Her expression was genuine. She took my hands in her bony fingers. Her skin felt thin, like my grandmother's. Marbella was, after all, an old woman. Despite her evening gown. Despite her boa. Despite her lipstick and rouge.

'Where do you live now?' I asked, trying not to feel ashamed for the whole night, for the kamikaze way I had accosted her, for being such a poor sociologist. Such a sloppy writer. Sociologists condemn us daily for our methods. But that's alright. I condemn them for theirs. Ever tried to read one of their books? More footnotes than actual text, which itself is so filled with fabricated Greco-Latinate words that you think you just stepped into the Roman Forum during Lupercalia.

'I live at the Knickerbocker. With all the rest of the old fogies.'

'I'm glad. I mean—' *Damn!* Open mouth, insert entire leg—'

'Ha! You're glad that I don't live on the streets like a nasty old bag-lady!' She seemed genuinely tickled. I relaxed a little.

'Will— you have lunch with me tomorrow, Marbella? My treat. *Musso & Frank Grill.*

'Such a gentleman. I'd be happy to have lunch with you, doll. I'd be happy to. We'll get one of Louie's tables.'

♪

Marbella Hutchins never met me at the famous grill on Hollywood Blvd. I went to the Knickerbocker Hotel looking for her, but the attendant told me in a typical Hollywood matter-of-fact tone, whether he was lying or not, that unless one of their elderly residents made prior arrangements, no one was allowed beyond the lobby, and they did not phone up for anybody not found on the 'call list.' So for several days running I went and waited in the lobby for her, hoping she would come out, hoping I would hear that she had been feeling just a bit under the weather or something. But I never saw Marbella Hutchins again. Not on Hollywood Boulevard. Not anywhere in the city. Not even in my dreams.

11

O'Neill

O'Neill lived next door to me, and two doors down and across from Margie—at the Regency. My room was sandwiched in between his and the one occupied by the skinny longhair who beat his gorgeous natural blonde girlfriend until I challenged him one night after I heard her beg him to please not hit her anymore. What would I do about that scenario today? Walk up to them, take her by the hand, and bring her to the safety of my room. Then, though, I was a kid who wasn't afraid, but wasn't much more than that either.

O'Neill had a girlfriend—a short, rotund, shocking raven beauty—who visited him sometimes. He played drums in a band fronted by a young woman who advertised herself as a lesbian; a band that was going nowhere really fast. He worked as a photography technician at some film development company there in Hollywood, and had all his nights free. He told me I could go in his unlocked apartment anytime when he wasn't there and drink whatever he had in his fridge—vodka, beer, juice, whatever. I think that was after the night he discovered he didn't have any food to eat and I made him some 'New England Clam Chowder' with black pepper, tuna fish, and 2% milk—and then made the mistake of telling him what I had used. I didn't drink alcohol anymore,[1] I told him, which made him laugh. I asked him why he kept his door unlocked. 'There's nothing in here to take,' he said with a shrug of his skinny shoulders and a quick mussing of his clean, flaxen collar-length hair. 'Go ahead. *Take* this old trap set, I don't care! I need new drums anyway. And I doubt anybody would want my kitty.' Basil, the cat O'Neill had brought to L.A. from his home in the North End of Boston, purred loudly when he heard his name, and ran to me. I had seen him a lot—O'Neill had lived at the *Regency* the first time I lived there, before I went back to Florida for those ill-fated months with the unorthodox Orthodox priest. That's a story for a whole other book.

---

[1] In my early 20s I had gone through a short period where I experimented with alcohol and marijuana.

Basil, a gorgeous solid black cat, put his front paws up on my thigh. I looked up at O'Neill, surprised. 'He wants you to pick him up and hold him—like a teddy bear. Put your hand under his bottom so he feels safe, and he'll stay in your arms until you put him down. I always did that when he was really little, and now he wants everybody to hold him like that. Go ahead. Try it. It's fun.'

I tried it. It was more than fun. It was deeply rewarding to have a cat, of all animals, act like a baby in my arms—like a live stuffed animal, a teddy bear. He was warm, he purred like a finely tuned engine, he licked my earlobe (I guess so he could watch my golden loop swing around), he nuzzled my neck. I loved the attention. I wanted my own kitten so I could train it like this. But the other part of me—the part that hates litter boxes and infandous hair balls and quick shadows making me jump—determined to never own a pet. This resolve dissolved for a few months in the summertime of 1991 with my cat Eliot and again in late 1993 with Jadi, but that's a completely different story—and life.

'Basil likes you. Why haven't you ever paid attention to him before, dude?'

'I've, well, I've always been a little afraid of cats. And dogs. Mostly cats, though, and big dogs. Not little lap dogs. The big kind. And cats. *All* sizes.'

'We all have our probs, I guess.' He sat down on one of his three metallic Adirondack steel folding chairs—the only furniture in his apartment besides the Murphy bed in the closet like we all had to sleep on (except for the paranoid longhair theologian-turned-drug-dealer-and-dog-breeder downstairs who had an antique four-poster bed, new wall-to-wall carpet, fresh paint, a new stove, and even a kitchen sink installed where the rest of us had to do our dishes in the little bathroom basin. 'Looks like you're getting over one of those little probs tonight. Good for you. Care for some suds? Got some primo juice here.' He popped open a bottle of Corona, inserted a wedge of lime, and reached into his fridge for another one. U2's album *Under A Blood Red Sky* played softly in the background—my all-time favorite recording.

'No thanks, O'Neill. I appreciate the thought, though.'

'Fuck me in the ass! That's right. Sorry, dude! I forgot you're sober.'

'Not sober, just a teetotaler these days.'

'Ha! I got to say, Sebastian, that's quite a feat, especially living here in Hellyweird. By the way, ever read any of that old sod Bukowski?'

'A little. Not much though.'

'I think your poetry sounds like him, except it's Christian. Hey, I know you don't drink, Sebastian (he always called me that for some reason), but do you want to come down to the *Carousel* with me, maybe have a soda while I get snockered on some good old rye? Classic old place from the Forties, I think. The bartender Randy's amazing to watch when he pours drinks four bottles at a time, and it's where Bukowski hangs out sometimes. He might even be there tonight. Want to come along?'

'Sure. Let's go.' I was always up for anything in Hollywood as long as I wasn't ostracized for not partying down with everybody else. For the most part, people were super cool about it. Tinseltown hosts all sorts, and teetotalers with a spiritual agenda, once recognized as such, are just another part of the eclectic mix. I was happy to be considered one of the freaks. And that popular Punk-Funk song was true. We really *did* come out at night.

♪

Bukowski wasn't at the *Carousel* that night, but Mickey Rourke, the actor who played a character based on him in the film *Barfly*, was. We chatted with Mickey for a few minutes—amiable guy. I told him that I loved his film *Angel Heart*. He said that he appreciated my compliment very much. Then he bought us drinks—I had a Shirley Temple. We chit-chatted a little more, then Mickey said he had to go home and prepare for his next role. 'You know, guys.' He stood from his barstool to leave. 'My grandmother always said that God has a plan for everybody. Well, I wish I had gone with his plan, because mine sucks. Oh, and, *ah*, Bastion or Sebastian. Whatever you go by, dude. Careful with them witches. *Angel Heart* was based on a real story.'

O'Neill looked at me sideways as Mickey left the *Carousel*. 'What's he talking about witches for? You doing something I should know about, Sebastian? Or *shouldn't* know about?'

'Ain't no thang, dude. Anyways, y'all Yankees ain't had witches up in your neck of the woods since Tituba's time.'

'Who the hell's Tituba?'

12

Ensueña

My shift at the Beverly Center bookstore where I worked—the one named after the famous pond where Henry David Thoreau built his cabin—was about half over. We had a steady trickle of customers, busy but nothing overwhelming. *Yet.* A book signing was scheduled for the next day, and that would make our already extremely lucrative store an utter madhouse—some semi-famous director signing his book about his extraordinary life in Hollywood which, I was sure without even reading it, was far more unusual and exciting than anybody else who had ever lived in Los Angeles before, or ever would again.

I had stationed myself at one of our two cash registers, where I always preferred to work since I disliked shelving books, when a striking young woman strolled in. Not that striking young women didn't stroll into the bookstore all the time, because they did. But this one was different. Unlike most young Hollywood hopefuls, she was dressed old-fashioned, wearing a calf-length cobalt blue dress and Menorcan sandals. Her only accessory was a clutch purse that matched the blue in her dress and her shoes. She was about five foot six with golden hair that not only sported a charming cowlick but also fell down her back in soft waves. Her lovely large grey eyes, framed by the Nordic version of the epicanthic fold, peered deep into mine. She smiled. Her teeth were perfect except for the front two that crossed over one another, making her that much more eye-catching. A classic and deeply attractive Hellenic nose and a muscular, nimble physique—complete with defined triceps—rounded out the vision for me rather nicely. My friend and co-worker Ronaldo leaned over to within my earshot and whispered, 'I like a sweet swayback like her.' Ronaldo was eternally on the prowl for a wife, and this redhead in the Romance books would do just fine, or maybe that Hawaiian dream in the Metaphysical section, or even the strawberry-blonde over there in the Religion & Philosophy area, or perhaps that beauty of a chocolate brunette in the popular Judaica reading material—it mattered not. She could be skinny, fat, medium, famous, unknown, rich, poor, Atheist, Christian, Muslim, Jew, contented, upwardly mobile, or fabulously successful—he didn't have a preference. 'As long as her face is beautiful,' he always said, 'that's all I care about.' I thought that was a pretty shallow approach to marriage, but who was I to talk? The girl of my dreams had to exactly fit the description of the one who had just walked in, or no dice. At least she was my model before I fell under the spell of La Mora. Then things changed, but I'll get to that later. What do humility and its opposite self-righteousness have in common? Only a little is required of either to make huge alterations in this weird dream we call *life.*

The beautiful girl in question approached our registers, but she was clearly not interested in Ronaldo. He slunk away like a cat caught in a sudden downpour and sat down in the managers' swivel chair, an assistant manager himself, and reluctantly finished off his *PayDay* candy bar—the kind of candy he always bought on payday. My 'sight for sore eyes' placed her superbly manicured and perfect fingers on the counter in front of me. 'Would you look up to see if you have the book *Hollywood Babylon?*

'We have it,' I replied cooly as I felt myself fall headlong into her eyes. All I could feel was a profound passion for her soul, an enveloping desire to know her, love her, be with her. 'Two copies all the way back, last shelf on the left, against the wall. Our Hollywood section. *Wait.* I'm not busy. Follow me and I'll take you.'

'Okay,' she replied as sweetly as any girl could ever say it. My heart beat faster than it had since I had last raced the city bus down Beverly Blvd. to get to the Beverly Center before my friend Nancy got there—just to see if I could win. And yes, in my newfound love of the pulchritudinous blonde walking behind me, I forgot to pray—for a little while anyway. Her pheromones, quite alive and directed at me, were just too overwhelming, and weak stupid burro that I am—

From Thanksgiving through the middle of January, if you volunteered to work the register you stayed there all day until it was time to clock out—unless you needed to leave for a minute or two to help somebody find a book. The stay-where-you-are thing was an unwritten rule, mind you, but one enforced by an unknown authority just the same. Sometimes this shift at the front could be a grueling 6 to 8 hours, most of your customers arrogant, in a hurry, self-important, rude, and self-important. It was so rare to host a person like the girl I was now helping—sweet, friendly, exuberant, stunningly gorgeous—yet reserved.

Our mall bookstore wasn't any wider than a broom closet, but it was as long as a football field. I exaggerate, naturally, but you get the picture. It took me and my future wife, I hoped as I whistled along, a half minute or so to get to the area where the book she had requested was routinely shelved. I pulled a pristine copy from the well-stocked shelf and handed it to her, as was our bookseller routine. 'Bastion,' she said, still smiling. 'I am Ensueña.'

My perception shifted so fast that I had to steady myself on an endcap. 'I see you already know my name.'

'*Deténgase. Nosotros te mataremos. Olvídate de nosotros.*'[1] As Ensueña said this, she handed the popular book back to me, turned, and left the store in as an unhurried manner as she had entered. In the months I had spent in Los Angeles, I had yet to pick up enough Spanish to understand what she said to me. I could say *cholo, que pasa, buenos dias* and *tardes* and *noches, nachos, burrito, quesadilla, taco, bonita, estúpido, chingala, puta,* and a few other words, but never enough to make a coherent sentence unless I was telling a Latin waiter what I wanted to eat. Or calling him stupid or a bitch, which is never nice in any language.

The next day—Monday—I was off work. When I went back to the job the following day, I asked Ronaldo if the pretty blonde had come back in. 'She may have while I was on lunch or in the back room doing something, but other than those times, no, I didn't see her. Wish I had though! What a knockout!' That was good enough for me, because not only was Ronaldo eternally amorous, he was a master of his surroundings. If he said he didn't see the most beautiful woman on Earth, then she likely had not come in.

A minute after I came back from enjoying a hot Reuben sandwich at the deli upstairs in the food court part of the mall, Ensueña strolled in. She was entirely ravishing, wearing a red dress similar in cut to the blue one she had worn. Her clutch purse and sandals matched her dress. Not at all knowing what she had said to me the day before, I still liked her, a lot, but I also felt nervous. What would she say to me this time? She walked up to the counter where I stood as

---

[1] "Stop. We will kill you. Forget about us."

the usual register sentinel who loved books but found their organization and shelving to be appalling—especially at minimum wage. Ensueña spoke to me, her eyes glimmering with an intensity I had rarely seen in any soul—almost a hatred, but definitely a challenge to battle. '*Deténgase. Nosotros te mataremos. Olvídate de nosotros.*' Then she turned and left.

A chill ran up my spine. I lost my joy. I felt my eyes glaze over—my whole face, really. I felt everything inside me wilt. Ronaldo, who happened to be near the registers again, asked me if I understood Spanish. I told him that I knew a little, but not near enough to decipher her words. He shrugged and went back to doing what assistant managers do, whatever that was. I had already been made a key-holder, and all I knew different about my job was that I had a key to the store and could open and close the front gate. I usually didn't, but that seemed to be beside the point. I also got with my promotion another $.05 cents added to my hourly pay. That would buy me 25 more packs of ramen noodles a week, or one cup of coffee upstairs at the sandwich shop where the bored, inattentive Latino girls normally sold me French baguettes with aged Asiago cheese melted over them, and day-old coffee—at my request because I didn't know the difference between aromatic dark blends and burnt java. In fact, I knew nothing at all about coffee, though I had loved its scent ever since I had first smelled it being roasted in New Orleans at the Folger's plant when I was really little.

I was glad that I had been raised Christian by half-hearted believers, had gone to a Baptist church filled with half-hearted believers, and had attended a private Independent Baptist elementary school run by half-hearted believers. *Why?* Because I knew that my fervor for God was not the result of my having been indoctrinated into their outwardly religious systems. In fact, all of my life, ever since my baptism at 9 years, I had watched with distaste the way Christians around me conducted themselves. God had personally revealed himself to me, and I wanted something far more, far deeper, far richer—and I knew it was available, if I could just find somebody to show me. Which, of course, made for a good laugh in Hollywood among my coworkers who would pat me on the back, dust the dandruff from my shoulders, and invite me over for a friendly game of cards or Trivial Pursuit or a rented VHS movie or something—all-time favorites being *A Christmas Story,* and *Parents* starring the bizarre Randy Quaid.

I failed miserably to see that I had every version of the Bible known to man at my ready disposal, and more than that, if I would nurture my prayer life instead of merely *talking* about nurturing my prayer life, God would reveal himself to me in even deeper and deeper ways. I knew the promises, I believed them, but it hadn't been really real to me—as real as I wanted it to be anyway—until I made the mistake which caused me to want to leave Hollywood the first time. During the course of those long months away, I realized that I alone was the grace-empowered pilot at the wheel when it came to setting myself apart for God's design. No one else could do it for me. It was me, and me alone, who had to go beyond mere desire and engage my will to love God above anything, and if I didn't do that, didn't pursue that life for myself, then I would suffer the consequences.

That night, as I dreamed on that creaky old Murphy bed, I was in the Mojave Desert. Purple rocks danced among red and orange ones. The sun had just set, it seemed, and as I watched, or walked—I don't know which—I saw three figures approach a fire which had been built near a huge natural stone formation that, as far as I could see anyway, created something like a cave or at least a three-sided shelter from the wind which now seemed to whip up from nowhere, bringing stinging sand with it. I awoke and looked at my red digital clock. It was 2:33 AM. That may not seem too significant, but '33' had for several years been important to me. It reminded me of the approximate age Jesus died and resurrected, and it happened often when I looked at clocks, especially digital clocks, to check the time. I used it as a way to know if I was on schedule with what God had for me to be doing at any given time. I still use the number that way, primarily with digital clocks. I have been using that exact same clock, a Spartus, to tell time for 30 years at this writing, and, despite multiple relocations from coast to coast, it's still going red and strong.

The next day I felt bleary; under attack by unseen things that maybe some people would call ghosts or memories or would just chalk up to depression. But I knew different. The two times I had encountered Ensueña had done a real number on me—especially after I deciphered, with the help of a Spanish-English dictionary, what she was saying. Would she come back and warn me a third time? A fourth? A fifth?

Would she push me into warfare with her and her witchy
lineage? Would I die at the hands of the most beautiful girl
on Earth? Would she give up, as Costanada seemed to have,
and leave me alone to whatever tactic would be revealed to
me to be rid of their influence in the world, or at least find a
way to warn people who were under their hypnotic sway?
Don had been dead on. Ensueña had indeed come looking
for me. Now it was up to me to pull their key from the
keyhole and lose it. But how?

I read the rest of the Arlo Costanada books over the next
couple of weeks, one after the other and in order. All carried
the same enticing, invigorating suggestion to take hold of the
world and force it—force Infinity—to give you freedom and
eternal life. This was true witchcraft minus the frills, thrills,
and chills of dancing brooms, haunted rooms, gloom, doom,
and wicked old witches trying to steal dogs from little girls.
Ever wonder why a Dunce cap and a witch hat look similar?
No? They are based on the same ancient design that has even
been found in the Gobi Desert of China on desiccated corpses
of Caucasians who lived and died there. The idea is that the
wisdom and knowledge swimming around above us can be
coaxed down to us here below by way of an inverted funnel,
through the point on the hat. Needless to say, Costanada and
friends didn't wear anything of the sort. Or, did they? *No.*
They were advanced *brujos y brujas* who dispensed with
outmoded methods of attaining wisdom. All they had to do
was to listen to the wisdom of the fanciful John Matanza and
the sorcerers of his assemblage, pick a few magic
mushrooms, prepare a concoction of peyote and jimsonweed
every now and again for that extra-special jolt into
Dreamsville, and all was well. And, I had to admit, the
knowledge they held sacred—the way of life—was certainly
captivating, and even compelling. But I knew that if I
continued on the path I had walked from a child, everything
I needed to know, and do in life, would be revealed in due
time. I asked God for the divine assistance to continue, and
often I would fall so low because of the internal pressures of
L.A. that all I could do was to cry out for mercy. It was *hard*
living on less than $5. an hour after taxes when rent every
month was nearly $500. and I still had to buy food, do
bicycle maintenance, and pay for a phone.

♪

Yes, Ensueña is dazzling and charismatic, I thought, but I bet Jezebel and Delilah were too. I hadn't seen Ensueña in a few days. Had she given up on her quest to stop me? I hoped she had, for my sake and for hers.

No such luck.

My next day off I found myself back on Melrose Avenue, my old and beloved haunt, dirty as it was. For Hollywood, there was a surprising lack of debauchery on that street, though. There were a few bars, one or two dedicated to the Gay crowd—and there was that one creepy bath house near La Brea, I believe, where when you walked past it you could hear groans and other noises coming from inside it—extremely hellish and unpleasant. I had been warned repeatedly not to ever go in there. I had taken the warning seriously. Overall, though, Melrose was filled with record stores, used clothing shops, and burger and falafel and ice cream joints. On this day off from work, I visited an artsy electric sign-maker's shop. He was kind to me—peculiar in Hollywood—and explained that he used neon, krypton, argon, xenon, and helium gasses, and even some mercury for that intense blue light seen in many signs. I asked him if he would apprentice me—as I have asked a number of people through the years—but he explained that I would need to go to school as he did in order to learn the 'ins and outs' of his particular trade. I told him that I understood, thanked him, and was on my way out onto the sidewalk, the popular local band *Guns-n-Roses* blaring out of the record store next door, when I saw Ensueña. She stood across the street in front of Double Rainbow, an ice cream shop. This day she was arrayed in a rich yellow—in a dress similar in cut to her others, which made her as ravishing as the other two times. But now my perception had been transfigured by her evil words, so I regarded her as one might regard a black widow spider—admiringly but at a safe distance. I looked at her for a few moments, and then, quite used to being aloof, I turned and headed west on Melrose. I had a date with a chili cheeseburger and some fries up the street a few blocks, and I was going to miss that like I was going to miss my own funeral which, thinking about it, I was accelerating with every single bite of that scrumptious, horrid food. I soon had the dreamy blonde out of sight and mind. My favorite

The Teachings of Don Luan

Jerusalem[1] tune played through my head almost as if I had it
on my turntable back at my childhood home in Pensacola.

I ordered my 'heart attack on a plate' and sat down at one
of the restaurant's shaded picnic tables. A homeless man
asked me if he could share my fries with me. I've always
loved helping the downtrodden, so I told him to come and
join me. The tough-guy Cholo cook at the window gave me
the eye for encouraging the local strays, so I gave him the eye
back and we commenced a brief staring contest until he gave
up and disappeared to nurse his deep fryer. *Jackass*. I'd bet
he found himself homeless not too long after that. At least I
hope he did. We all need harsh lessons sometimes.

My transient friend was not only friendly, but a
gentleman. He only ate a handful of my fries, and then tried
to pay me with the few quarters he had been able to gather
that day. I brushed his money away. He nodded and smiled.
'Thank 'ee,' he mumbled, nearly toothless, as he turned and
lumbered away into the heat of the day. I sat there for a few
minutes in rapture at having been able to help feed a fellow
sojourner. Then I felt eyes boring into me from behind, so I
looked up, half expecting the greasy burger flipper to still be
challenging me because of my heinous kindness in the City of
Lies.

When I finished eating and was ready to leave, I looked
up to get my bearings in a city that still tilted and turned and
flipped upside down for me like some kind of giant robotic
toy. Ensueña was standing there gazing at me—no emotion
at all. She stood with her feet together and her arms by her
sides. 'How did you find—' I began but then stopped because
it is fruitless to ask this sort of question of the consciously
godless or the determinedly godly, either one. Both have
magic, both can make serpents from staves, but the latter's
reptile eats those of the former—every time, no exceptions to
the rule. Armed with this truth, and also knowing that
neither I nor Don nor anybody else who hated witchcraft
were trying to keep others from expressing themselves but
rather halting them from hurting the unwary, I stood from
my picnic table and boldly walked over to the ravishing
beauty who had made it her recent life's work to incessantly
confront me. We must have been a picture of youthful
loveliness, the blonde and me, because a handsome

---

[1]   A Metal band from Sweden.

photographer who had also been having lunch—chili cheese fries as I remember—whipped out one of his several cameras and snapped a series of shots. Ensueña turned ferociously away and hid her face while she screamed at him that she would call the police for harassment if he didn't bring his roll of film to her that instant. As with all photographers I have ever known or heard of, he calmly cased his camera, shook his head as if to say 'What an arrogant twat,' walked over to his Rolls, and sped away down Melrose, headed west. I looked down at my ripped faded blue jeans and then back at Ensueña's teal midi with matching Menorcan sandals and hair barrettes, then back at my sleeveless designer t-shirt. Then I shook my own head. Ensueña turned back to me, her beautiful fingers still covering her face. I sensed that she wanted to ask me if the photographer was gone, but that would have blown her witchy cool, so she braved a look around and, satisfied, resumed her stance against me. *Wait a minute,* I thought, suddenly disoriented. *Wasn't she wearing yellow when I saw her just an hour ago?*

'*Deténgase. Nosotros te mataremos. Olvídate de nosotros.*'

What was I supposed to say in response? I just stood there and looked at her. She was a bit less pretty when she took the present approach, but I was still enamored with her. I couldn't see Ensueña as my enemy no matter how hard I tried. I knew that my fight wasn't against flesh and blood, and this made me love her and pity her. Yet, I also felt very strongly that she meant every syllable she spoke, even if they fell like feathers against my combat boots. I wasn't afraid. My hope was in something far greater than threats from a coven of witches. I had a reckless berserker of love on my side, and he was making me into a berserker of love just like him. All I needed was more prayer, more patience, and the divine help to make no occasion for my flesh to act in accordance with the ways of the world system. If I said any of this to Ensueña, would she even know what I was talking about? I talked about it sometimes with Margie, my friend three doors down at the Regency. O'Neill listened patiently when I broached the subject, but I could tell by his look that he had not a clue about what I was saying. Ronaldo and my other 'politically correct' coworkers thought I was just some kind of Deep South relic to brag about—like they had discovered an oddity they thought had completely disappeared from the face of the Earth sometime in the early part of the 20th Century, if not much earlier.

'*Deténgase. Nosotros te mataremos. Olvídate de nosotros.*'

There. Ensueña said it again. Then she turned and walked away, but as she did so I thought I saw the glimmer of a smile play about her lips—the kind of smile that says I know you're not the least bit afraid, so this whole thing is making me feel a little self-conscious. I hoped I had read her expression right, because if I had, I'd have her sandcastle demolished in a matter of days. There was still a part of me, though, that did not at all like the fact that she could find me anywhere in Los Angeles I happened to be. Venice Beach for a Saturday afternoon stroll through Freak Land? *She was there.* Malibu for something deliciously different than the filth of Tinseltown? *She was there.* Hollywood Boulevard on a Friday night for a movie feature at the Pantages Theatre? *She was there.* Beverly Blvd. on my way home from a shift at the bookstore? *She was there.* Even riding an impromptu midnight city bus with my bus driver friend through Downtown L.A., Watts, Compton, and then back into Hollywood? *She was there.* It was enough to make me scream the 'Wilhelm Scream' time and again. *Aiiiiiuhh!* And believe me I did, which seemed to amuse Ensueña, but you'd have to be really good at reading the infinitesimal vibrations of eye pupils to see it. A little something I learned as a pirate when I was eight.

14

80s Girl

Letter to the Girl with the Golden Curls:

I was a bookseller at the Beverly Center in Hollywood. It was late 1989.

You routinely came in. You were absolutely beautiful. And you had the thickest head of golden brown curls I had ever seen.

I loved you. You loved me.

So after a few of your visits to allegedly look at books, I decided to say hello. I was excited. So were you.

Of the five Love Languages, yours must be the same as mine: Words of Affirmation.

'Your hair really freaks me out,' I told you.

The sunlight quickly faded from your eyes and face. 'My hair freaks you out?'

'Yes!' I said, trying my hardest to let you know that I meant my words in a positive way. 'That's an old 1970s way of saying I like it.'

You didn't believe me. You were an 80s girl, not a 70s girl. 'My hair freaks you out—' you said, even sadder now. Tears welled into your eyes. 'My hair freaks you out—'

'No!' I said. 'Really! I like it! I like your curls!'

You turned away from me and never came back into the bookstore.

And I've missed you ever since.

I hope you are well, and still excited about life.

I still love your kinky, playful, 'Shirley Temple Gone Crazy' curls. (I met her once— in that same bookstore!)

I'm no longer available. Happily married. Not at all lusting after you. Just remembering.

Remembering your girlish smile. Your joy.

Yes. That's it. Your *joy* in Hollywood—a place where joy is rare, and true love is even rarer.

♪

Well, the sadness described in the above letter had just happened to me five minutes before when, after weeks of harassment, Ensueña came back in the bookstore, found me at the register (to my utter dread), and asked me for a certain book in the religion section. I knew we had it. We had lots of Bibles. I also knew it was her way of getting me away from my coworkers at the register, one of whom, of course, was Ronaldo.

When Ensueña and I were hidden away somewhere between *The Devil Is Alive and Well On Planet Earth* and *Strong's Exhaustive Concordance of the Bible*, she took, as if acting in a film, some nondescript volume from the shelf, turned to me, peered profoundly into my eyes, and said, with no expression on her pretty face whatsoever, '*Deténgase. Nosotros te mataremos. Olvídate de nosotros.*'

Unbeknownst to myself at the moment, and likely Ensueña, I was ready with a reply for the fair-haired beauty this day dressed in a pretty cornflower print with matching bag and black patent leather sandals from the same island as her others.

'*Los verdaderos seguidores de Jesús no tienen miedo. La muerte es un alivio para nosotros. Cuando Dios nos da trabajo a hacer, lo hacemos porque no tenemos miedo a la muerte. Mátame si quieres. Si se supone que debo vivir como la luz contra brujería, seré resucitado de los muertos.*'[1]

Ensueña stepped back from me, her lips parted in surprise and evident wonder, her eyes suddenly filled with admiration and, yes, tears. She fumbled with the trade paperback in her hand, and soon dropped it. I dutifully picked it up for her. She brushed it away. 'Shelve it again, please. I— I have waited for someone more potent than that control freak Arlo to appear. I want what you have—a *real* relationship with God, not some weird connection with something called the Eagle or Infinity which, of course, only he and his sex-charged ways can bring to me—or any of us women. Will you show me how— to come home?' She took

---

[1] "True followers of Jesus have no fear. Death is a relief for us. When God gives us work to do, we do it because we have no fear of death. Kill me if you want. If I am supposed to live as the light against witchcraft, I will be resurrected from the dead."

me by the hand, began to weep, and walked me back to the cash register.

I felt myself go hot around the collar. I loosed my skinny red 80s tie. 'Were you testing me, you silly New Age poofball?'

She seemed to be genuinely humbled. 'I wasn't testing you at first, no. After a while, yes, when I saw that you weren't afraid. I was sent by Arlo to *remove* you. He fears you, as do the others. As I did. Until just now.'

I forgave her, against my better judgment which I had already learned was my worst enemy.

Ensueña smiled through fresh tears. 'Can we have coffee sometimes?'

'I'd like that, Ensueña.'

'No. My *real* name is Aaron Sunderland. I'll go by that from now on.'

♪

When God answers prayer, he really answers prayer. Ronaldo was so envious he playfully snapped at me for a week while he demanded that I give him every detail about my new friendship with 'that perfect girl who came in and wanted to talk only to you, schmuck. Some guys have *all* the luck, ya schlong!'

I always really enjoyed it when Ronaldo, just five years older than me, got upset or mad about something because it was just like watching a character in a movie from a much earlier American era come alive—like somebody from the 40s or 50s maybe. Mad but not *really* mad, you know? Just sort of miffed. One time I was convinced that I saw steam shoot out of Ronaldo's ears.

15

Starlet

Why don't we ever listen? Why did the crying, terrified girl who begged me and my friend Skee Goodhart to help her that day in Central Hollywood listen to the ghetto fool when he told her that he was a movie producer? With his 300 pound muscle-bound ape standing right next to him? Who was *he* supposed to be? The director?

Skee wanted to call up to our friend Hank in the old gated apartment building and have him buzz us back in. Skee wanted to save the prostituted starlet. Skee didn't live in Hollywood. *I did.* I saw the two freaks aforementioned as they waited next to the 'producer's' shiny black BMW. I saw the 'director' reach deep into his double-breasted suit coat, laughing silently like Satan. When Skee and I passed them, because we *had* to pass them in order to get to the convenience store on Hollywood Boulevard where we were going to buy potato chips, the 'director' said in his demonic bass voice, 'Good choice!' The 'producer' mouthed expletives as he swung his fifth of vodka and fought to keep himself from munching asphalt. I pray the girl got away from the Demonic Duo, but chances are she didn't.

16

Sherri

What could Sherri have become? She rented a stale, semi-furnished apartment at the Regency, a two-story building of a score of rooms, ten on each of its two straight red carpeted and chandelier-lit hallways, five rooms on each side. The place had been built for starlets in 1941, and at that time only starlets could have the rooms. There may have been space for a small refrigerator, but when the Murphy bed was pulled down out of the closet (where no clothes could possibly be hung) there was barely enough room for the couch and maybe a chair if you were lucky. Sherri told me that she heard from the old man who lived in a back apartment upstairs (Don Luan, of course) that both Bogie and Marilyn Monroe had once lived at the Regency. But that was a long time ago, and she wasn't too sure who Bogie was anyway. She knew Marilyn, though, but her idols were Madonna, Heather Locklear, and Jennifer Jason Leigh. It's why she had moved to Hollywood. No one told her, though, that she really needed to have trained as an actor, that she really needed legitimate contacts in Hollywood, that she really needed an acting coach and fan base back home, and that she really shouldn't sell her sex to wanna-be Rock stars (guys in their 20s who dressed in skin-tight spandex, wore their hair long or had extensions, plucked at second-hand electric guitars, and claimed to be in this or that up-and-coming 'Rock-n-Roll Phenomenon,' dude!).

Who could Sherri become in this filthy, poisoned-air city? She was a natural blonde, and she had a beautiful, athletic shape with no obvious needle marks—if there were any to begin with. She always seemed clearheaded enough, if perpetually sad. And not the Hollywood perky-lipped and puppy-dog eyed 'I'm so sad' either, which, more often than not, is acting when acting is neither called for nor being paid for at the moment. *No.* Sherri carried the real kind of sad that made her a little talkative, but not much, and keenly interested in the boy upstairs who professed with youthful *naivete* that he was still a virgin after she asked him one night if he had a girlfriend.

Sherri didn't like anybody knowing that she made her rent every month by 'entertaining' other Hollywood hopefuls.

The Teachings of Don Luan

Not many in the building were interested in her story anyway, because there has always been a severe lack of leisure in Hollywood for anybody whose goal is to actually survive its deadly onslaught. Small towns and suburbs provide their inhabitants with ample time to pry into the business of others. Cities dwelt in by untold millions, most of whom live paycheck to paycheck unless they are the girl we presently observe (and hopefully with some compassion—for indeed she was a very sweet-hearted soul), provide only an atmosphere of desperation and disapproval for even the most talented aspirant, whether he be an actor, writer, director, makeup artist, musician, gaffer, photographer, or any one of the other nameless masses who relocates to Hollywood to work in the 'Biz.' And then there are the raving craze-eyed lunatics—and possibly even demoniacs—who moan and curse and talk to graffiti, wads of greasy paper, invisible people, street curbs, walls, friends who have died, and lampposts. And don't forget the grinning weirdos who walk down Melrose wearing infant underwear as hats, a jar a petroleum jelly in one hand and a copy of *Playboy* in the other. Okay, I only saw one of those one time, but it still disturbs me.

Sherri knew that she would never be an actress three days after she got to Hollywood, but she couldn't go back home. She wondered how long her self-centered mom and third stepdad would believe that she had become a 'working actor'—after, of course, she had explained what one was.

'You ain't famous, stupid girl! I never seen you on the damn TV!'

She explained that working actors sometimes only do local commercials never seen by anybody outside of the Southland, meaning the Los Angeles Basin and surrounds, but they couldn't have cared less. They never believed she would amount to anything anyway, and revealed their philosophy to her on a daily basis from the time she was old enough to understand words. Before that, their words just sounded mean and hurt a lot. But Sherri watched lots of TV and only had sex with a few boys in middle school and only a few more in high school and with that one boy in the bathroom at Big Daddy's Lounge who was from New Jersey, but she held on to her dream of moving to Hollywood and making it big and finally being proud of who she was for a change.

The Teachings of Don Luan

The first week in L.A. was a disaster. Sherri got her apartment at the Regency the same day she got off the Greyhound, which was easy enough to do. She was pleased, though, to have a place to sleep and eat her ramen noodles and peanut butter (though she had to do her dishes in the tiny bathroom sink), and she liked that most of the people who lived in her building were budding Rockers, because she loved Heavy Metal and it was, after all, the 80s. Why couldn't she party a little bit on the side? Isn't that what you do in Hollywood when you're not working?

After Sherri was settled in, she went to her first casting call. She left there crying because a girl about her age asked her where she had gone to school and she said Robert E. Lee High where the boys from *Lynyrd Skynyrd* went to school, which prompted the more seasoned actress, with contained thespian sarcastic glee, to ask where *that* was, and when she replied 'Jacksonville, Florida,' well— that was Sherri's first and last casting call. She was smart enough to know she couldn't now do what she had fantasized doing since she was eleven, but not smart enough to use protection that last time—though all the guys in the building whispered about her being 'clean,' and now she had an abortion on her conscience as well as everything else that hovered over her sorry life like a vulture waiting for a wounded animal to die— a small wounded animal with big blue eyes and a heartrending 'Meow.'

It helped the virgin boy who lived upstairs (yours truly) none at all for Sherri to want to see his apartment one evening. Armored as he was with his stolid virginity, it was still painful and exhilarating for him to follow her 5'2 barefoot frame up the spiral stairs from the first floor after he saw, quite clearly, that all she wore was a t-shirt which barely covered her *derriere*, emphasis on 'barely.' After she said 'I feel so dirty,' turned away, displayed her wares directly in front of him, and placed her hands on her cute bare knees to look at his Christian music cassette collection as she exclaimed in her sweet voice 'Christian Rock?' he nearly gave in to her incessant verbal (yet always coy) attempts to help him 'lose' his virginity. He told her in an effusive hormonal blurt that she could use his shower if she wanted to. He told her this three times in quick succession, hoping she would turn and ravish him like a raging warrior-queen until his brains spewed all over that decrepit roach-infested flea-ridden 1970s-ripped-avocado-shag-carpet apartment. A hellish Heaven or a heavenly Hell. At that point it mattered not to him which.

It wasn't long after that close-call incident—only a matter of an hour or less—that the virgin was grateful beyond words that Sherri had glanced at him sidewise, smirked at his utter lack of arousing manhood at the moment, and left his apartment, still dirty, with a giggle and a 'Bye-bye, see you later, virgin boy.'

Did she ever 'amount to anything in life'?

17

Bob

Bob Haggard was the Regency on-site manager. A big, muscular, forty-something brute of a man who wanted to be a kind, selfless man but also a self-righteous tough-guy *brujo*. One is going to win out over the other every time. *Brujería*—witchcraft—requires an absolute focus on selfishness in order to work. And, our world is filled with witchcraft—of all shapes and sizes. Most of it, though, is never detected as such, but the wounds and scars it causes are as damaging, and often as deadly, as the recognized version.

When Bob found out I was a writer, he located an old electric typewriter from one of the vacant rooms—there were a few in the building, likely because screenwriters with broken dreams had discarded them there when they left town wailing into the night—and brought it to me to use if I wanted it. I took it, but not until after he sat down in the hallway just outside Don's apartment and across from where the gorgeous woman lived, the one who came to the door when I was talking with Don that one time. Bob began pecking away, with no electricity, at the keys, pulling and tightening the archaic ribbon, flipping the keys (some of which were broken), and doing a general not-sure-what-I'm-looking-at maintenance on the discarded machine. When he seemed satisfied, after having given me quick glances and a word or two to tell himself that he was in an actual conversation with me, which he most certainly was not, he got up and said 'It's yours,' and left. During this grueling process, because I was exhausted and needed sleep, the beautiful woman came back to her door, obviously disturbed by Bob's deep growl of a voice. She smiled weakly at me, as before, and then softly shut her door, as before. I wondered if she was a high-end prostitute. She was certainly equipped to fit the bill, and why else would she be living in this old, forgotten building if she wasn't incognito? I guess I was born to be a writer, or a detective. Maybe both, which is probably why I adore Raymond Chandler. I also love dry humor, and Chandler offers it in spades.

The Teachings of Don Luan

I picked up the old typewriter. The ink ribbon and machine oil greeted me anew with their familiar scents. I was suddenly thrown back in time.

My father was fond of taking me fishing on Stone Lake in Century, Florida where we'd fish for bluegill bream[1] and catfish. I had to be real quiet, though. I couldn't scuffle my feet in the boat. And I couldn't talk either. A whisper every now and again was alright, but it had to be about fish. And not just *any* fish. I liked sharks, but those were off limits while freshwater pole fishing. I told everybody I wanted to be an chondrichthyologist when I grew up. They usually just smiled and looked over at whichever parent was present, usually my mother, who would smile back and shrug her shoulders as she basked in the bookworminess of her peculiar little boy.

My father was a hunter, even when he was fishing. He exemplified the strong, silent type. Once we had slipped out over the weedy green waters and were stalking our unseen prey, there was no horseplay nor idle chit-chat allowed. We were there to *fish*; to master the elements; to bring home not one or two denizens of those murky waters, but a whole string; a freezer full, which we would clean and freeze in plastic milk cartons against the unforgiving wintry months when cold showers are preferred to fishing on cold, windy lakes. (I didn't like all the bones in the fish my parents ate, nor did I like the smell of fried fish, so I always had fish-sticks instead.)

One cool October morning, my father and I went fishing without a boat, so we 'borrowed' one from a fisherman who wasn't there. I was really worried about that, but my father said it was okay, as long as we brought it back in the same condition we had found it in, or better. *Or better*? He taught me to scull with the paddle that day, and said I did real good. I felt proud.

The next weekend we took a long road-trip out to an old concrete well that my father had drunk out of when *he* was a boy. I felt excited about that. The way he painted the good old days, I longed to go back and spend time with him when he was a boy; run through the woods with him; hop trains with him; work at the Pensacola docks heading shrimp with

---

[1] pronounced 'brim'

him. *Anything*. I didn't care. Just as long as I could spend time with him.

When we got to the wooded area where the cement well was, we realized we hadn't brought anything to drink out of. But on the rim of the well sat a tall wax paper cup somebody had left. My father said the sulfur in the water would kill the germs, if there were any to kill. That sounded right to me. When I think of those moments in the cool 'fishing weather' breeze of that morning, I can still feel the icy water burbling down my throat. I can still smell the strong scent that was a little like rotten eggs, but not too much. That day we also found some wild scuppernongs.[1] While we pulled the meat out to eat, we checked to see how far we could spit the skins and the seeds. My father won, but he was a lot taller than me. His went soaring yards away. Mine only went a few feet.

Not long after my sculling adventure on Stone Lake, I learned how to drive in our brand-new '74 Impala. My father took me to part of the Old Spanish Trail. He was long-suffering with me as we sped along haphazardly in that 400 horsepower monster across big clumps of grass and uneven red bricks which I imagined were being quickly lain down in front of us by Spanish soldiers who hoped we would be patient enough for them to finish their job. Decades later I was to read somewhere that the famous road was actually begun in 1915, to connect New Orleans to Florida, and extended later to connect Florida to California. Sometimes it's just better to never learn the truth—if that *is* the truth anyway, which I doubt.

A year earlier, to the day, (it was my birthday) my father had taken me to an 19th Century farmhouse ruin in the backwoods of railroad and steamboat town of Pollard, Alabama—famous for never having allowed prejudiced people to live there. There as we moved carefully through the old boards with nails in them, I found a hand-made brick. Then a rusty nail went through the bottom of my tennis shoe, so my father had me take my shoe and sock off so he could check my foot. It was slightly punctured, but it would be okay, he said, and it was. My father said I could take the brick with me, as a souvenir. I proudly covered my birthday surprise in cellophane paper so it wouldn't wear away. For years I used that brick as a doorstop in my bedroom. The last

---

[1] A kind of wild grape with a thick indigestible skin.

time I ever saw it, sometimes in the mid-80s, the paper had been taken off it, and it lay next to the house in our backyard. That discovery made me sad, but looking around the house I had seen built from the cement slab up in the early summertime of 1970, lots of things made me feel sad.

A few months after my driving escapade along the Old Spanish Trail, my father and I went to another part of the woods near Holt, Florida and stumbled across a briary pig-trail running through a tract of land filled with long-leaf pine and oak. That day my father showed me the difference between water, white, red, live, scrub, and Spanish oaks; and taught me how to call like a bobwhite as well as a whippoorwill. We also found an old door laying over a pile of sticks and trash.

'Hey, *hey!* Look at *that!* Wonder what's under *that!*' my father cried. He was always a little boy again when we went out on adventures in the woods. We had stopped bringing my little sister Patsy after the very first time. She hated the woods and stood at the head of the trail and cried until my father got so disgusted with her that we got back in his fishing truck and drove straight home— at least 60 miles.

'Careful about snakes,' I warned my father as I stood frozen, waiting for him on the very safe pig-trail. I just *knew* he was going to get bit. I wasn't *about* to go out in that jungle! He kicked at the old rotten door, stomped on it a few times, and then stood up and waited.

'See. That's what you do, Bastion,' he said. 'It'll run any ol' snake outta there, but you gotta make some noise.'

'What *kinda* noise?'

I was imagining the biggest rattlesnake in the world. Fangs as big as the fingers my father playfully jabbed at all us kids, pretending his hand was a snake head, calling his fingers 'fangers'.

'Noise like I just made. Weren't ya watchin' me?'

His voice was serene. Very kind.

'Now, them ol' water moccasins,' he added. 'They're another story *altogether*. They won't move when you make noise. No sir. You have to get a ol' stick or somethin' to move 'em with. A long one, though. They won't just bite you once. They'll bite you 'til you're dead.'

My adam's-apple was stuck in my throat, and I didn't even have a fully grown one yet. *Bite you 'til you're dead!*

'Hey-*hey!* Look-a'*here!* Look what we got *here!*'

I was halfway back to the car.

'Where you goin'?' my father asked me. 'Come on back here! Look what we found!'

What *we* found? *Hmmmmm—*

I crept gingerly back down the shady path until I got just behind my father. I was still expecting a snake, a dead snake, a thousand baby snakes, a snapping turtle— something dangerous.

But no. My father had found us a 1920s typewriter. Man, he was so proud of that thing! So while I watched out for rattlesnakes, he moved all the debris and sticks and the door which had been used to cover the machine. We loaded it up in the trunk of the car, took it home, and cleaned it up with some of his brushes he had gotten from NASA when he had worked for them as an aerospace engineer in New Orleans.

The next day we drove into Downtown Pensacola and ran down a ribbon at an out-of-the-way typewriter shop. This was one of those places where the friendly men talk about fishing and old-model cars and the good ol' days. I breathed in the clean, rustic scent of lubricating oil and leather. The store smelled like the barber shop and the shoe repair store in Flomaton, but nothing like my Uncle Paul's bait shop in South Flomaton where we got earthworms and crickets and blood bait. The crickets were the worst—millions of them in a huge lidded box. Sometimes my Uncle Paul would have me go back to my maternal grandmother's house and pick thick light green or black catalpa worms off the catalpa bushes he had planted on the side of her house. At first I was scared they would bite or sting me, but after my father told me they wouldn't, it was fun looking for them on the broad lime-flesh colored leaves they lived on and ate.

The men working at the repair shop were nice. One of them showed me the inside workings of a typewriter. *The flywheel. The gadget flip. The jam-keys. The thumb-snap. The finger-pinch. The paper-rip.* And, of course, the ribbon we had come to buy. My father laughed good-naturedly. The men all smiled and called me a fine young man.

As I would sit pecking away on that machine into the wee hours of the morning, typing up my poetry and stories, I knew that I would make my living as a writer one day.

Not only did my father give me a love for people, he also gave me a burning desire for exploration which has taken me around the world, and through many a forest. I hope he is proud of the woodsman I have become; that he always hoped I *would* be.

Not long ago he went fishing with some of his boyhood buddies. He'll be back for me one day, though. He needs me to scull the boat.[1]

---

[1] A type of rowing done with one oar at the stern of a small boat so that the result is like the tail of a fish moving back and forth through the water.

18

England

His name was England. Well, his *real* name was Brand
Tissue, but he preferred England for some unknown reason.
He was my first friend in Hollywood. He played drums in a
Heavy Metal band called 'Happy Cat.' I don't think they ever
made it big.

England was from Anaheim. I had been to Anaheim. I
had not liked Anaheim, and I told him so. 'I stayed at the
Ivanhoe Inn one night,' I said as I stared down at Mary
Pickford's hand and footprints at the Chinese Theatre.

'So that's why you don't like Anaheim,' he said. 'Now it all
makes sense. C'mon, Bastion. I wanna take you somewhere.'

'Where's that?'

'The Beverly Center.'

'What's that?'

'The mall for this quadrant of the world—if indeed L.A. is
on Earth, which is debatable. We'll take a bus. It's on the
border of Hollywood and Beverly Hills.'

'Can't get mall life out of your system, hoh? Were you a
mall rat growing up?'

' Trust me. There'll be hot chicks there.'

'That's all I needed to hear, England, because there aren't
any hot chicks anywhere else in Hollywood.'

'Fuck you,' he replied with a broad smile, his red-hair-
dyed-pink cascading down over his skinny shoulders like
spilled Hawaiian punch. 'Got bus fare? I'm flat broke, dude.'

'How do you eat then?'

'With my teeth. What else, my asshole?'

♪

The Beverly Center was anti-climactic. There were a few
pretty girls, but most of them were with their pretty
boyfriends. We took in a movie—can't remember what it was,
but some blockbuster from 1988—and then headed into a
giant store.

'The *toy* store?'

'Got a problem with toys, Bastion dude?'

'Dude? Don't call me *dude*, man.'

'It's what we say here in the Southland, ass-wipe.'

'I prefer *dude* over *ass-wipe*, I think.'

England grabbed a plush stuffed dog off the shelf and made it turn its head really fast and look at me. I laughed so hard I thought I was going to fall down. Then I grabbed a stuffed cat and did the same thing. England *did* fall down. The cute girl behind the register laughed with us. I think England had 'smoked up' before we left Central Hollywood. Funny thing, he never asked me if I wanted any. We just hung out and laughed and looked at girls and movie stars and laughed some more. He tried to get me to watch the movie *Weird Science* with him, but I wasn't interested. 'Me and my roomies watch it every night. I've seen it seventy-five times and counting, dude.'

Then one day, after I played a wildly popular joke on England's roommate and band guitarist Mike and used his private phone number to advertise in the local musicians' rag that a new rap-metal-funk-polka band was forming 'with a lemony peppermint twist,' and after we all laughed long and hard about it, I never saw England again.

Sweet-hearted England. A good boy from Anaheim—behind the 'Orange Curtain' where, at this writing, prescription drug addiction, crippling, and death—witchcraft in yet another form—is a pandemic.

Unlike so many people in Hollywood, England didn't want anything from me except my friendship. My friendship in a lonely, unforgiving city. I guess I'll always miss him. Even if he did shout 'Hey mother! Want another?' to every pretty girl who strolled by with a baby in its stroller.

19

Rufus

Rufus was the paranoid longhair theologian-turned-drug-dealer-and-dog-breeder who lived downstairs, just below me, at the Regency. I could see his door from an odd little balcony that was between O'Neill's room and the next one down—which I believe was empty. Across from that one was where Margie lived, usually on her Murphy bed depressed with just a candle burning or her dim bathroom light. She liked it when I went to see her. She could be cranky without her coffee, though, as I discovered one morning when we drove across the city in her exhaust-coughing, rumbling bluish green '65 Falcon to eat breakfast at a relatively inexpensive buffet. I was 'hopped up' on life and ready to talk! Margie wasn't—until she had her first few sips of that bitter drink I hated so much at the time, even with loads of sugar in it, and sometimes milk or even chocolate syrup to try and mask the horrible taste. (What could I have been thinking? Perhaps it was the fact that at that time in L.A. to ask for 'good coffee' was like asking for 'safe heroin.')

Rufus invited me to 'kick it' with him at the *Carousel* one night, so I went along, as I had with O'Neill, for the laughs. This night Charles Bukowski *was* there, but he looked like he wanted to be alone, or just talk to Randy the bartender, so we let him have his space. After all, his celebrity was based on anti-celebrity, ironic as that is, so, in a way, we were fostering his celebrity by letting him live the Hollywood anti-celebrity life he wanted to live. Hilarious if you think about it.

'I was raised in a Southern Baptist home, in Sandusky, Ohio.' Rufus took a sip of his whisky on the rocks. 'Not many Southern Baptist churches up that way, but our family was devout. As I got older, I became even more pious than my family members and fellow parishioners—if you want to call them that; my fellow churchgoers—so that all I wanted to do was to devote my whole life to ministry of the Gospel. I wanted to pastor a small church, like the kind that still has the graves outside in the churchyard. You know, the old-timey wooden white churches with the tall spires and the cross on top.'

I nodded to show that I knew what Rufus meant. I had all my life been a real pastoral romantic, loving graveyards and old churches and historical places, be they forts or houses or barns—it mattered not to me. And on top of all that, most of my family was buried in the mostly forgotten graveyard of an old, unused white church with a tall spire. 'So what happened?'

'Ever hear of Pacific Christian College? Down in Fullerton?'

'I have a good friend who goes there, so yep, I've heard of it.'

'Well ain't that a coincidink! *Ha*! Who'd of thunk?' His blue eyes flashed in the dark. He seemed delighted. I couldn't help but chuckle. This longhair drug dealer was still a white-bread Christian underneath all his tough streetwise veneer.

'Well, against my parents' wishes, and my pastor's, I didn't even apply to SBTS—the Southern Baptist Theological Seminary in Louisville. I applied to, and got accepted by, PCC, where your friend goes. I took my Bachelors, and then in three more years made it all the way to my Master's exam. The big day finally came. My advisers and I sat in one of the school's boardrooms over coffee and donuts, and they began the oral exam. About halfway through I stopped them cold. Want to know what I said?'

'Sure. Tell me.' I knew he was going to tell me anyway.

'I told them, I said, 'You know, your Christianity is a fucking crock of shit. I'm convinced after watching you all for all of these years that Jesus was just a man after all, like any other man, and this whole shebang has been designed to deceive the masses.' Well, my main adviser, Dr. Thornton, after a few moments of shock along with his prestigious colleagues and my secondary advisers, stuttered until he found words enough to say that though he appreciated very much my wry cynical statement on the way the *world* sees Jesus, he thought that perhaps I shouldn't have used gutter language as part of my delivery, and if I would apologize, or at least plainly show how my satire was relevant to my impending degree, he would be happy to move on with my exam. I was the one who felt shocked at that point. I screamed 'No! You don't get it, do you, you pedantic piece of theological garbage! This is what you fucks have taught me since I've been here all these years at your goddamned school! I came here as a lifelong devout believer in Jesus Christ, who at that time I called my Lord and Savior, and your system here at PCC has done nothing but place doubt in my mind from day one! In a way, though, I actually owe you all a load of gratitude, because you have opened my fucking eyes to the total bullshit that Christianity is, and always has been! Oral exam over!' I stood, knocked over my chair, and stormed out. Back at my room, I packed my things, called friends I had hooked up with over the last year or so of school, and moved here to Hollywood. Business has been boomin' ever since. You need something by the way? I can get anything you need, and I do mean *anything*, Bastion. Just name it, friend.' He stirred his whisky with the little red swizzle stick sword and took another swill. I took the sword I had out of my Shirley Temple and read what it said along its blade: *Sword and Shield of York*. 'Look at this!' I cried, trying hard to feel relaxed after his bombshell of a story. 'Look what it says.'

He picked his sword up off his bar napkin. 'Now *that's* fuckin' weird!' He shook his head in disbelief. 'Only in Hollywood, dude. Only in fuckin' Hollywood do you get a reference to Robin Hood floatin' around in your ice cubes.'

'And in Yorkshire,' I added. He had to stop and think about my dry sense of humor for a second. I could see him trying to make something deeper out of my words than what was there, but then he guffawed as if he had just been told the funniest joke in the world and sucked the last of his drink down. 'Keep 'em comin' Randy!'

'One sittin' here for ya right now, chief. And another Temple for the lady.'

My head shot around to the bartender. Randy just stood there, a semi-silhouette in front of all the back-lit bottles of yellow and gold and transparent liquors behind him, grinning at me like a chessy-cat,[1] waiting for me to say something aggressive so he could tell me to get the hell out of his bar. He knew Charles Bukowski was watching, and I knew he knew it.

Rufus jumped up from his leather booth seat. 'He's joking, Bastion! It's his way of sayin' he likes you. Give me a couple bucks and I'll tip him for you. I've got the tab for tonight. Pay me back later, or whenever you can.'

I pulled a five out of my wallet and handed it to Rufus and nodded, trying to show that I had swallowed the offense I

---

[1] The Deep South pronunciation of 'Cheshire Cat.'

felt. 'I need to get goin', dude. Got an early day tomorrow for work. See you back at the ranch some time. It was fun.' As I was leaving the *Carousel*, I stopped at the bar, sucked the Shirley Temple down in a swallow, patted Bukowski on the shoulder, then shot Randy a friendly smile. He stopped drying the glass he held and gave me that weird, broad grin again, glad I could take his gruff street-level humor without getting mad. 'Cool old place, man,' I said with a quick wave in his direction, and I was through the swinging cowboy saloon doors and back out on the Boulevard heading west down the polluted spit-and-gum-covered sidewalk. I was soon dead to the world, laid out on my Murphy bed which I normally left out of the closet for convenience. I'll leave you now with a Bukowski quote:

'Some people never go crazy. What truly horrible lives they must live.'

20

Fritz

I should probably preface this chapter by saying that Don Luan told me that one day I would need to write about the people I met while I was living in Hollywood—that I would learn a lot through remembering, and that the wisdom I desired would eventually develop from that knowledge. There was no plant-picking-and-preparation with him, no discussing an amorphous infinity, no aimless wanderings at night through desert chaparrals, no elaborate practical jokes, no being chased by enormous insects or teaching mothers they can become virgins again or shot at by crazy witches on rooftops or gazing into space to discover animals from 40 million years ago that could still kill me if they wanted to. None of that happened with Don Luan, and I'm grateful. Why? Because wisdom can't be taught—it has to come from experience. And not drug-induced experience, either. My life experiences have proven to be far wilder than any drug I have ever heard of.

When I was in cosmetology school in Pensacola back in the mid-80s, there was a Pensacola Jr. College student who came in early one morning before class to have his long black hair cut.

'Just give it a little trim,' he instructed me as he pulled his faded green Army jacket closer to his thin frame, as if it were colder in the salon than in the chill outside.

I began to do as he asked.

'Those look sharp,' he said of my hair-cutting shears—the ones I had paid $100 for, which was astronomical for those times.

'They're sharp alright. I cut myself pretty often on 'em. What's your first class?'

'English Lit. I'm a freshman. I know I don't really look like a freshman. That's because I'm twenty-three. I fished for crab in Alaska for a few years. I thought it'd be fun. It was, and it wasn't. It was hard. I'll tell ya that much. Hard and risky.'

'Sounds interesting,' I replied as I snipped here, snipped there. I was envious. I had never done anything at all. I had never been anywhere except three week-long church camps in the summertime, a week-long cross-continent church mission trip from Florida to Lake Erie, one or two weekend church trips to Alabama, *Disney* when I was 11, and Puerto Rico for a week with the family at 13. The rest of my experiences in life were relegated to interesting conversations with students who attended Pensacola Jr. College.

'You into Punk Rock?' my new hair client asked.

'Oh yeah,' I replied less hardily than I felt. My heart thrilled. The Punk subculture meant everything to me. Angry, aggressive middle-class kids screaming that their lives had been ruined by this and that and the other, mainly their parents. Today, it all seems so silly and irrelevant. Then, it was what I lived for— while refusing to be a part of the burgeoning Punk scene in Pensacola, mainly because I didn't drink, do drugs, or have sex—except for the short while I tried the first two.

'You act like a Punk Rocker,' the guy said. 'You're kinda tough and cool at the same time. You're kinda—*scary*. Like you might be a witch, or maybe a witch-finder.'

I felt both empowered and freaked out. *Witch? Witch-finder?* For the empowerment part, it didn't take much to make me swell with pride in the browbeaten days of my youth. I mean, this little, wiry fellow who could pass for a seasoned AWOL soldier or a well-traveled European was saying that I—a boy found mostly in a world of poetry and dreams and Christian rock music—was *scary*.

'We're the same age,' I said as I undid the shiny brown nylon cape from around him and shook off the cut hairs.

'I guess you're getting a late start in life too. Thanks for the haircut. It looks great. My name's Fritz. It's Norse.' He handed me two dollars as a tip and stepped out the door into the cold wind, unbuttoning his jacket as he went.

♪

Two days later Fritz came back in. His hair was the exact same length as it had been before I cut it. This time as I trimmed his locks, the conversation was a bit more surreal.

'You ever fished for albermagon in Pensacola Bay?'

'What are albermagon?' I had never heard of this fish.

'Albermagon taste a little like catfish, but not really.'

'I like friend oysters and fish-sticks, but that's about it for seafood.'

'Albermagon taste like oysters too. You ever lived in Los Angeles?'

'No.'

'You will,' Fritz stated matter-of-factly.

'What do you mean by that?'

'Oh, nothing really. Only that one day soon you're going to be living in Hollywood, California. That's all I meant.'

'That is a really strange thing to say, man.' I couldn't help but laugh. Fritz laughed along with me, and said nothing more on the subject. By this time I was fairly used to strange people saying really odd things. It was Pensacola after all. A place that, to this day, I really despise, but that's neither here nor there when it comes to the absolutely bizarre conversations one can have with seemingly normal people in that town. There's something in the air—or the water.

As I shook the thin nylon cape out again, long black hairs flying everywhere, Fritz tipped me two dollars as he had done the time before, unbuttoned his Army coat, and walked out into the freezing January morning.

'Bastion?'

'Yeah?' I turned to the voice of one of my female cosmetology classmates. It was Susanna.

'Bastion, that guy you just cut— he came in three times last week. And every time, his hair was the same length. I cut it all three times.'

'Really? That's just weird.'

'You're tellin' me.'

♪

The next morning Fritz came back in for another haircut. His hair was halfway down his back. I felt nervous about that.

'Haircut?' he said. 'You can take most of it off this time. Just leave me a long bang in the front. That'll look cool.'

'Sure you don't want a tiger stripe mohawk or something?' I wanted to mess around with bleach and color for a change, plus I needed the color credits so I could graduate.

Fritz's eyes grew wide with childlike glee. 'Can we do that?'

'Sure,' I replied, excited to do something different than permanent waves (which I was no good at) and hair trims.

'Let's get your mohawk cut first, then we'll mix up the bleach and get it lookin' cool!'

I cut Fritz's hair the way he wanted it, and then left him there for a few minutes while I went to mix the color. But when I returned, he was gone. The girl running the appointment desk said he left me two dollars along with the regular cutting fee our school charged, which wasn't much.

Fritz never came back to the salon again.

Two years later I saw him walking down Hollywood Boulevard. Yes, the one in California. I wanted to say something, but he was too far away, and I didn't want to yell. Anyway, I was late for work.

21

Molly

Blood and chocolate were smeared across the dingy white wall of the empty Regency apartment down the hall from my room. I needed the faded, stained, decade-old red velvet couch some designer had thought was a good idea once, so I ignored my terrible ideas about what had happened in the room, and, without getting Bob's permission, took the furniture. I never went back in there when the place was empty, though the door was always open.

Later I was told by long-time resident Don Luan that about a year before I moved in, an unmarried couple had lived in the room—a bartender and his stripper girlfriend. One night they engaged in a loud argument, and in the process Molly, the girl, grabbed Jeb's hunting knife and cut his throat. When the police got there, she was sitting cross-legged against the wall near the window facing south toward Hollywood Blvd. She was eating a box of chocolates Jeb had bought her for Valentine's Day. As she stood up to be cuffed, so I was told, she casually wiped her hands on the wall. 'Blood and chocolate tastes good together,' she was heard to say. 'Messy, though.'

After hearing that, I examined the velvet couch closer. Horrified by what I found, and already having moved it into my room, I stuffed it into my large closet I never used and tried to forget about it. But I couldn't. I never had any bad dreams. I did, though, begin to write a story, or maybe the beginning of a novel, about a girl gang leader named Molly and her life in a dystopian Hollywood after hundreds of thousands of American youth stormed L.A. and destroyed the city's infrastructure. Street gangs marauded at will, with no resistance from the relatively nonexistent authorities. The story never went anywhere, and one day, during a fit of lunacy, I destroyed what I had written.

♪

'Don—'
'Say no more, Bastion. Come in, come in.'
We sat in Don's sparsely furnished room—seems like every room in the building was sparsely furnished except for

the ones lived in by Bob the manager and Rufus the drug
dealer who had spent thousands of dollars updating his pad.

'Coffee's good, Don. Thanks.'

'Cool out, hot out, coffee works both ways. You'll get to
like the taste one day. I promise. So, tell me what's
happening.'

'It's just all too much. My calling to attack sorcerers, the
city itself with all its wiles and weirdness, the women always
after me—and even men. *Everything*.'

'Cursed with good looks, I see. Well, there's worse things.
Try being good-looking and born a eunuch at the same time.'

My mind whirled. 'Are you saying what I *think* you're
saying, Don?'

'I think you get what I'm saying, but it's worked out good
for me. I've always been able fully concentrate on God, never
having the problem of being sidetracked in the least bit. I
believe if I had personally been born normal, you know,
down there, my life would have been far more difficult than
it has been.'

'Yeah. I can see that. *Heh*. I experience it every day. The
women just won't stay off me! Everywhere I've turned since I
was about fourteen, there they've been. Pothead chicks,
cheerleaders, church girls, prostitutes who want to give me
freebies, quiet poetic types imagining marriage, upwardly
mobile mall store managers with uncertain designs—you
name it!'

Don smiled sadly yet joyfully—a rare combination. 'So tell
me, Bastion. *¿Qué pasa?*

'It's just all too much, Don. Too heavy.'

'True that. It *is* too heavy. Without one of three things in
your life.'

'And those would be what?'

'A true love and desire for God, or money coming out your
yin-yang so you can do as you please, or a numbing
desperation mixed with full sobriety. Any other attempt to
placate this monster of a life never works. Many, many find
out the hard way.'

'So, let me get this straight. I either love God and do his
will and let the cards fall where they may, or I figure out a
way to step on people's heads so hard that the money flows
like a bloodbath, or I stay away from booze and drugs and
desperately make myself a numb cog in the wheel of 'the
Biz'?'

'That's about the size of it—except that the last two are only temporary fixes that lead straight to Hell anyway. You know, Bastion. You didn't have to come back out here to Cali.'

'Yes I did.'

He smiled, wisdom shining all around him. 'Why's that?'

'Because it would have been disobedient not to.'

'Good answer. So how 'bout them witches?'

'You know Ensueña?'

'Sure do. Or *about* her, anyway. We've not yet met.'

'Like to?'

'Thought you'd never ask, Bastion.'

'You knew, didn't you.'

'God tells me the latest, especially when an indomitable witch with a murder streak gives her life back to him—*and* gets the boy! That's important news in *any* gazette.'

'I'll bring Aaron by tomorrow, that alright?'

'*Aaron*. A nicer ring than *Ensueña*. And yes. Tomorrow is fine, say 4 o'clock? I look forward to it.'

'Speaking of murder—'

'Molly and the dystopia story you've begun, inspired by the creepy empty room next door?'

'You amaze me, Don.'

'And God amazes *me*. So, it's the least I can do to amaze my fellow servants. Call it a gift. Anyway, about tomorrow. I'll make the cake. You bring the ice cream. It's her 27th birthday, you know.'

'I do now.'

22

Tucson

'I was hiking in the desert just outside Tucson. It was wintertime, and so beautiful.' Aaron wiped a few tears away from her face with the back of her hand. 'So simple with just the rolling orange sands and saguaro cactus everywhere I looked.'

Don handed her a tissue. 'Why are you crying?'

'Because I loved Jesus so much back then.' With these words she broke down and wept, agonized with the remorse that always comes with those who have been called personally by God and then have turned away because of some fleeting earthly glamour—witchcraft being, for many, the most delicious of all available fruits.[1] As Don put it so well, without a burning love for God, an availability of money gets us through, and if we don't have money, then sobriety coupled with an insensitive desperation is the remaining choice—but how many people can be filthy rich, or actually choose desperate sobriety and can maintain it for any length of time? The fourth and last option, one that Don didn't mention, is suicide. The world is filled with far too many drugs, of all shapes and sizes, and not all of them are physical. I haven't yet mentioned my brother Jabbo, and I probably won't again, but his drug has been, for the last half century, pure envy. Envy is what keeps him going, what placates him and gives him a strange hope in himself and his talents. A bizarre drug indeed—and, apropos to any study of Hollywood because it is one found time and again in the writings of L. Frank Baum[2] where beautiful Dorothy Gale is concerned.

---

[1] Witchcraft was the *original* sin of Adam and Eve, being really nothing other than the false belief, based in self-pride, that we can be autonomous gods in our own right, that we have no need of connection to and communion with our Creator and Source. There was only one Tree in the Garden. The forbidden 'Tree of Knowledge of Good and Evil' was the knowledge of God not yet 'ripe' as it was on the 'Tree of Life.'
[2] Author of *The Wonderful Wizard of Oz* (1900).

The Teachings of Don Luan

♪

Aaron seemed to be enjoying her chocolate birthday cake, which she had mixed up in her bowl of vanilla ice cream. 'Okay. I feel better now. Well, I was hiking and taking some pictures. I love photography. I felt safe out in the desert like that, I felt God's angels all around me. Then I heard singing—some of the most beautiful singing I had ever enjoyed. It was a woman, so I followed her voice until I saw her. She was kneeling on a hill. She seemed old to me only because of her gray hair, because as I got closer to her, her skin was firm and beautiful. I could tell right away that she was Mexican. I introduced myself. She turned to me and smiled, and I fell in love with her, right then and there.'

'You mean, *ah*, sexually?' I said in one of my stupider moments.

Aaron was gracious. 'No, Bastion, not that way. More like, this is my teacher—I just know it. She knows things. That event threw me completely off balance, and I gave in with a surrender to the world that I never knew was inside of me. I had been so solid and unswerving in my love for Jesus, or so I thought. But my actions proved me to be quite a different person. So, anyway, the woman told me her name—Mama Tilo.'

I gasped. Another name Costanada warned me about on the day he nearly had a brain aneurysm because of my determined resolve to stop him and his cohorts. I felt dumb for gasping, but neither Aaron nor Don seemed to care, so I let myself slide and refocused my attention back on our new friend and, as I have said, the very model of womanly beauty for me.

Aaron sighed and shut her eyes for a second, evidently not really relishing the telling of her story but knowing that it needed to be confessed. 'Mama Tilo asked me if I would like to visit her *hacienda* sometimes. I was so excited I could hardly speak. I told her that Christmas vacation was coming up and that I had no family near me to spend it with. Could I come and spend a few days with her then? She let me know immediately that she was happy about that idea, and so that's what I did. Her map directions were perfect. My *Road Atlas* got me to *Casa Brillante* directly and with no confusion whatsoever. Her *hacienda* was a few miles outside Nogales, but still on the American side of the border. I say *was* instead of *is*, and you'll know why in a minute.'

I stood. My legs were tired. It had been a long day for me already. 'Can I make a suggestion?'

I was raised in a tough exurban neighborhood with red clay roads and the meanest kids you'd ever want to know. I developed a gruffness as part of my personality, and in my younger years it was hard to control. I blurted things out I shouldn't have, and made suggestions when they weren't appropriate. This was one of those times yet again, though I also have a soft heart cohabiting in there somewhere— hopefully softer as the years go by.

I cleared my throat a bit louder than necessary. I felt the heat of embarrassment creep up my neck as I began to speak. 'I think we should start fresh when we all feel good. I'm feeling a little antsy right now.' I believed then that Don would softly reprimand me, but he didn't. Aaron looked sad. I knew it was because she had hoped to be able to tell her story to us—*to me*—that night. She needed to confess. She was new again at this game—the 'God-game,' you might call it. The 'salvation game,' if you will. She had been gone from us for over a decade. She had threatened my life on quite a few strange occasions. And I was sure she had done some other things which would have been considered untoward even by the crustiest persons in Hollywood. Witchcraft offers those kinds of oddities where plain old day-to-day perversity has no idea they even exist.

23

Mama Tilo

I didn't want to confuse Aaron, so, against my hormonal drive, I told her straight out that we should be brother and sister first, and then let God develop something naturally between us if it was his plan to do that. She nodded. I could see that this idea didn't fit with her own plan any more than it did mine. But we hugged—not for too long, though, thank God—and she finally said it was a good idea, but that she did want to spend time with me, that I and Don were all she had right then. I told her that my phone always had its answering machine on, and also that she could come by anytime unannounced. In retrospect, that wasn't a great idea at all, given our amorous feelings for one another, but as it would happen, she never came by unless Don was also available to hang out, and that probably saved us from situations that we would have rather not found ourselves in just then. But do keep in mind that I was still pure as the driven snow, so me losing it to Aaron would have been an event similar to her trouncing a world-class boxer in tip-top shape.

♪

'So, Bastion, I mean, like, *wow*. You were on my hit list less than two weeks ago. This is just too crazy!'

'Welcome to *my* world, Aaron. And to my favorite pizza joint. *Raffallo's.*'

'Here comes the waitress.'

We ordered a large pizza with everything on it except green bell peppers and the little sour yellow ones. I was happy to discover that we both really liked anchovies.

'I want to—I need to tell you what happened, Bastion. How I got trapped by Arlo and Mama Tilo, and the 'Three Witches' Celia, Delia, and Emilia, and Regario Nostrali, Millaya Johnson, Kiki Willow, the man-cougar Goliath, Cordon Grey, and Henri Avelar. Oh, yes. How could I possibly forget La Mora? They are not—none of them—what Arlo says they are in all of his books. There was never really a John Matanza *per se*, or a sorcerer friend who once journeyed to Ixtlan and also helped to teach Arlo. No one in the group is anywhere near as magical or interesting or exciting as he or she is presented. Very little Arlo says has ever really happened.'

'What do you mean by saying there was no John Matanza *per se*? Or no Geronimo Juarez?'

'John Matanza, as he called himself, was an independently wealthy cast-about Arlo met one day in a bank lobby in West Hollywood. John had dabbled in some Hopi and Yaqui ceremonies and had also read a lot of Timothy Leary and Ram Dass and other so-called 'enlightened' Western teachers of Far Eastern thought. Arlo took a real liking to John, and so they began to hang out and discuss different topics, typical of people in the comfortable classes who don't have to work for a living. One day, though, Arlo heard through a mutual acquaintance that John had suddenly died. This was back in the early 60s, and so the John Matanza legend was begun, or I should say, the sorcery lineage.'

'Well, should I be surprised by any of this really?'

'I thought you might be at least a bit surprised that most of it is lies—especially since one thing about them—about us when I was with them—was, and is, *impeccability*. An impossible feat for a fallible human—a tightrope act that makes you crazy after a short while. But a word pregnant with integrity and honesty, wouldn't you say? '

'Your impeccability I *did* notice. You had me terrified, Aaron. I felt like Elijah sitting under the broom tree asking God to take me home, terrified of Jezebel. I didn't know when you were going to show up next! How did you do all that?'

'All of what?'

'Know exactly where I was, when I was going to be at home, or work, or strolling down Melrose or hanging out at Venice or taking in a movie on the Boulevard or catching a band at the Whisky[1] or whatever.'

Oh! *Ha-ha!* Well, I guess I should tell you. I have a Master's degree in Criminology and, when I met Mama Tilo, I was set to join the LAPD police force as a rookie Detective here in Hollywood. I kept the police friends I had when I left to work for CG & Co., Arlo's community relations arm. So, a quick phone call, my identification, and a good description of you and the patrolmen told me exactly where I could find

---

[1] The club Whisky à Go-Go on Sunset in West Hollywood.

you. You have to admit that a guy who wears his hair really short and rides a sky-blue mountain bike in Metal-Head Hollywood would be a good start for the officers. And then there was that one other little thing.' She smiled impishly. 'I would just call your bookstore stock girl Kristine or your manager Bradley to find out if you were working that day. One time I think I also talked to your assistant manager Ronaldo. That was the guy at the register with you, right?'

I rocked back on my heels. 'You have *got* to be kidding me!'

Aaron lowered her eyes. 'Do you still trust me?'

'No dammit!'

'I understand—' She moved to leave the restaurant.

I took Aaron's hand. 'I was kidding you.'

'It didn't sound like it.'

'I was raised in Ferry Pass.'

'What's that, the Compton of Northwest Florida?'

'No, that'd be Brownsville or Warrington. Ferry Pass would be comparable to— you know, there just *is* no comparison— that I know of anyway. The people are middle class and poor class all mixed together. Lots of paper mill workers and Navy retirees, Monsanto workers, house painters, barbers, auto repairmen, hairdressers, plant operators, store clerks, plumbers— all kinds of blue collar people. The light of God is the only thing that gives some of them any hope at all. The rest just live their lives like they're slaves waiting to die.'

'They *are* slaves, aren't they?'

'Yeah, I guess they really are.'

'There's— just one thing that mystifies me about you, though, Bastion.'

'What's that?'

'I had no idea—nobody told me and no records show— that you speak Spanish.'

'I *don't* speak Spanish. Or any other foreign language for that matter.'

Aaron's eyes grew wide. 'You mean— I mean, you're telling me that—'

'I guess that's what I'm saying. Yep. Looks like witches ain't the only ones who can turn rods into snakes.'

'You— you were speaking a language you don't know—like in the *Book of Acts*?'

'Appears so, Aaron. So, I have an idea. Why don't we eat and then go back to my place.'

'Bastion!' She playfully slapped my hand.

'I thought I might get that reaction out of you! *Ha*! What I meant is, I'd like you to meet some of my friends in the building. Then maybe, if it's not too late, we can go hang out with Don and you can finish your story about meeting Mama Tilo. I'm off work tomorrow. By the way, have you found a job yet?'

'Surprise! I start *here* as a waitress tomorrow. Our waitress Lisa interviewed me this morning. Her daddy is the owner. Lisa told me not to be surprised if I get big tips, because this place is one of the best kept secrets in Hollywood. She said the other night some man gave her a ten dollar bill as a tip, and all she did was to bring his pizza and cola out!'

'That's a super nice tip for sure. So, whaddaya say, li'l lady? Have our pizza then head back up the street to ye olde Regency? Oh, look. Here it comes now.'

As Aaron introduced us, Lisa lit the candle nestled in the pan warmer—one of *Raffallo's* signatures, the other being that they have a completely open kitchen where they cook right in front of everybody. No swearing or getting mad there! Good for the atmosphere.

The pizza, as always, was superb—a sumptuous, oily medium crust flavored with just the right amount of salt and a smidgen of garlic for that mild sting always complimentary to all other ingredients—except for maybe orange slices like they do in Ireland. Aaron said she loved it and hoped we would come back to eat there again. I promised we would. I tipped Lisa with a twenty and left her standing there smiling a silly smile. As we walked out the door, I saw her go to her daddy and tell him what had just happened. He shrugged congenially and said something to his daughter, but I didn't hear what it was. The next time we ate there, though, the pizza came out with a plate of Shrimp Fettuccine Alfredo— probably something somebody ordered and didn't want, but still, it was a nice gesture, and proof to me and Aaron both that she had already won favor at her new job. And the money? I've never known a waitress to make so much moola in my life. And, Aaron observed, it was a lot safer, and more fun, than being a police officer in Los Angeles.

♪

'So, I have a surprise for you both. I hope, anyway.'

Don sat up in his chair. 'I'm excited. Tell us.'

'Well—' Aaron rolled her 'well' out for almost ten seconds according to the clock on Don's wall. Just another cute thing about her, her childlike way about things. I was amazed, and still am, that she was ever planning to become an officer of the law. 'The surprise is— I'm moving here, to the Regency! The 'blood and chocolate' room, right next door to you, Don, and upstairs here with you both! Bob was quite a gentleman.'

Don sat back and lay his arms on the chair rests. 'He's that way with *all* the ladies, if you know what I mean, Aaron.'

I was staggered at the news of Aaron moving, pleasantly so except for the fact that it was the 'blood and chocolate room', and I'm sure my face beaming pink let her know how I felt about her relocation. Her rent would be far cheaper than it had been in the Fairfax District, and she could now walk to work at *Raffallo's* in a matter of just a few minutes instead of having to drive. I looked over at Don for a second. He nodded and raised his eyebrows as if to say, *You surprised, young man? She loves you.* I took Aaron's hand to reassure her. She gripped my fingers like a baby. I was glad she trusted me—and I was frightened at the same time.

'I am taken aback, though,' Aaron added, 'about one thing. I had no idea whatsoever that La Mora lives here at the Regency—some kind of undercover thing she's doing, I guess, as part of her perception expansion. We met each other in the hallway out there. She looked at me blankly and then turned and went inside her apartment. I didn't get the feeling that she has any plans to harm me in any way. And, I now have guardian angels again, if they ever even left me at all, so I'm not worried.'

I shot up out of my chair, spilling my ice tea all over my lap. '*Who* lives here? Did you say *La Mora* lives here? *The* La Mora? The *witch* La Mora?'

'Let's not go out, *um*, until that dries, alright?' Aaron joked. 'It'll look, you know, *funny*. Like you had a little accident or something.'

Her levity worked. A bit, anyway. I sat back down and looked at Don questioningly.

'I figured you'd find out at the right time, Bastion. We always do.'

'Well, who *is* La Mora? Which room? That petite blonde downstairs with the Blues guitarist boyfriend? I know it's not my friend Margie, or that Rocker guy's girlfriend Kylie. Oh, no. Don't tell me! *Really*?'

Don sighed, a look of quiet satisfaction painted across his features. 'Yep. You got it. *Her.*'

Aaron touched my knee. 'You know La Mora, Bastion? I mean, you've seen her?'

'Yes, dang it, but we've never met.'

'Hope you don't. I mean, don't ever, *ever* go in her room, or even talk to her more than maybe a little 'hello' or something. She's a beautiful spider with only one thing on her mind—*power.*'

'I promise. I mean— okay, I won't.'

Aaron giggled and seemed to relax. 'Alright. Well I guess you'd both like to hear about Mama Tilo's *Casa Brillante*?'

'I'm all ears,' replied Don as he swirled his drink and sipped it. 'Want some more tea, Aaron?' Then he glanced at me. 'How 'bout you, Butterfingers?'

That hit Aaron's funny-bone. It was a minute or two before she could stop laughing enough to continue. Finally she looked from Don to me, back to Don, then to me again. Then she leaned back on the couch where she sat, took in a deep breath, locked her fingers across her tummy, and began her story.

♪

'The first room of *Casa Brillante*, nearest the foyer, was more than gigantic, it was unparalleled. Its walls were salt white, and mahogany rafters that ran across a cathedral ceiling seemed to emerge from gorgeous, flowery Art Nouveau wood molding the same shade as the walls—or lack of shade. From these rafters hung gorgeous crystal chandeliers that dated back to the 'Gilded Age' of American opulence. The floor was made of Nouveau-flourished glazed red tiles, each one about a half foot square. I was so taken by the majesty of the place—the *palace*, really—that I felt for the plush chair directly behind me and sat down, overwhelmed. Mama Tilo was gracious towards my amazement. She beamed, clapped her hands three times, and in a few minutes a petite, sweet-faced young woman dressed as a classic maid—black dress, white apron, white bonnet—came whisking into the room through an ornately carved swinging door. She carried with her a large silver tray of refreshments—a variety of sliced fruits like cantaloupe and watermelon, colorful nutty sweetmeats, and a delicious and refreshing ice-cold lime drink. Mama Tilo introduced us. 'This is Celia Durante, my maidservant.'

'*Maidservant*? That sounded to me like something out of an earlier century. Later, after we had chitchatted about school and general American culture, Mama Tilo set her fine china cup down in a most ladylike manner, her little finger poking straight out and everything, and said that she needed to disappear for a while, but that the entire house and gardens, which were dazzling to look at, were all mine for exploration to my heart's desire. She added that Delia Minchin, her chambermaid, would show me to my room, and then she asked me if I would stay for the whole college Christmas Break. I was ecstatic, and happily agreed to do so. With that, she disappeared. It was soon dark outside, but plenty of illumination was afforded by the chandelier lighting that I found could be controlled by porcelain rotary dimmer knobs. Three other knobs controlled the bass, treble, and volume of a variety of available music styles. I picked Soft Jazz and was soon soothed almost to sleep by Hadley Hockensmith's virtuoso guitar playing. Scents of jasmine mixed with juniper reached and comforted me even moreso. I read from several books of classic Irish and English literature for a while—some Yeats and Wordsworth as I remember—and then I chose to turn the lights completely off, recline near the glowing hearth, and enjoy the magical star-filled desert vista that several humongous picture windows offered to me. I felt prompted in those moments to pray, but then again, why? Wasn't my life a prayer already? I didn't know at that time that I was already slipping quickly into an unforgiving pit from which only the help of God could save me. Intelligence and suave in others had always been my weakest point, and *magical* intelligence was a death knell to my soul forever starved for artsy conversation and delightful shared observations of the aesthetic world around us. I wasn't long in my musing, though, when I sensed another presence in the room. I turned, expecting to meet the chambermaid Delia who would come to show me to my bedroom, but I went cold all over when I found no one with me in the vast parlor which, though a good fire still burned, was now far too large and shadowy for my sense of well-being. I got up quickly and walked to the massive window in front of me, which was the middle one of three the same size and shape—giant rectangles. I located the moon and then, further up and out, the stars of the Northern Cross. *Good*. I was still on Earth. I smelled cinnamon and chocolate just as I heard a rustling behind me.

'Miss Aaron?'

'I wheeled around. 'Delia?' I said to a gorgeous round-faced woman. She was dressed in a blue floral muumuu and wore matching rubber flip-flops, but everything about her was immaculate, her raven hair falling thick around her shoulders. She said that yes, she was Delia, and asked me to come with her, but first she would sit with me and have Mexican hot chocolate and crisp cornmeal wafers, which I found were only slightly sweet to the taste but went nice with the cayenne and other spices in our cocoa. We talked about the night and the desert cold and the beauty of it all, and then she led me to my room decorated in whites and pinks—canopied curtained poster bed, dressing table and mirror, matching wardrobe, the works. My dreams that night were all in black and white, oddly, and filled with memories from my childhood, good and bad. I was raised by parents who were never able to escape their own terrible childhoods—it's called, as I remember, 'arrested development.' It's one of the things you learn in several of the Human Development classes you're required to take along a Criminology course of study because field studies show over and again that most criminals, especially the violent ones, experience 'arrested development' in some shape or form. The most heartless people—serial killers, for example—are never allowed to play as children, but are given plenty of chores and, in some cases, lessons in dance, music, art, whatever in lieu of being able to playact with other children. Anyway, when I awoke, I smelled breakfast. After freshening up with an old fashioned pitcher of water and a basin, and, to my surprise, having to use a chamber pot in such modern surroundings, I found my way down a different set of spiral stairs than I had gone up the night before and into a dimly lit hallway which led directly to a spacious dining room. Two places were set in the middle of a long dinner table, one on either side. A tall girl with attractive long, oval facial features stood by the chair that faced yet another picture window. After she pulled that chair and helped me to be seated, she disappeared for a moment, but soon rolled out a cart filled with platters of fried eggs, bacon, cornbread muffins, whole wheat toast, churned butter, heavy cream, sliced kiwi and pineapple, strawberries, and a pot of black chocolaty-tasting coffee. 'I hope you're hungry, sweetheart,' she said, and smiled as she filled her plate higher than a lumberjack would. 'I am Emilia Blodmonath,' she said. I had to forcibly pull my eyes away from watching her cram food into her mouth like it was going out of style. She was talkative while she ate and said that she was on Christmas vacation from her fun, star-studded retail job at Giorgio Armani on Rodeo Drive. Studying her lumberjack mannerisms, I didn't believe a word of it. Later, back in my room for a quick power-nap, I used the 1950s-style phone next to my bed and made a call. It was true. Emilia Blodmonath did, in fact, work at Giorgio's on Rodeo Drive, and was on her 16-day Christmas vacation at *Casa Brillante*, a vacation won by having served them since their opening in 1964. This information floored me, because there was no way this tanned, pretty, twenty-something girl could actually be somewhere in her late forties. At this point I wasn't sure about staying at *Casa Brillante* for too much longer. I was already feeling a bit out of the water, and where had my host Mama Tilo gone? There was a reserved but kindly gardener who only said 'hello' when he saw me wandering through the rich, breathtaking flowers and plants. There was a handyman who always seemed to have a trowel or a hammer or some kind of repair tool in his hand. He was friendlier than the gardener, but still kept his distance from me. To my alarm at first, there was a pet cougar who just roamed around the grounds like he owned the place. But when he came up to me, in the presence of the gardener, and treated me like any other friendly house-cat would, I lost my fear of him. These three later became better known to me, of course, and I'm sure you've read or heard about them by now: Cordon Grey, Henri Avelar, and Goliath the sorcerer-cat. Well, I decided to stay on a bit longer, maybe a day or two at most. I had come in my own car, following Mama Tilo in hers, so it wasn't like I was trapped or imprisoned there or anything. Anyway, the day after I met and had breakfast with Emilia, Mama Tilo came back from wherever she had gone to. She greeted me warmly, asked about my stay, and then told me that five of her closest friends would be arriving later the next morning, that she had a huge party planned, and that she wanted me to be her guest of honor. I was floored with her kindness. For whatever reason, I felt like I needed this kind of love and acceptance in my life, so I readily let her know that I was excited to meet her friends, and that I had already enjoyed meeting Delia, Celia, and Emilia as well as the gardener and the handyman. She asked me if I had also met Goliath, and I told her yes, but that it always took me a while to get used to pets—especially man-eating ones.

'Oh, Goliath isn't a pet, Aaron, and he doesn't eat people either. He's a dear friend of ours.'

'I felt a little strange because of Mama Tilo's answer at first, but took it in stride and followed her inside because, she said, supper would be ready and on the table. It was. Roast beef with potatoes and carrots, a delicious split pea soup mildly spiced with cayenne or some other kind of hot pepper, a stack of piping hot white corn tortillas, pistachio yogurt dip, and coffee with shortbread for desert. While we ate, the gardener Cordon came and played a lovely, soft violin—and one time I giggled to myself because I couldn't help but think of the hilarious response to anybody who complains about anything in life: '*The world's smallest violin, playing the saddest song, just for you.*' Mama Tilo looked up from her plate in curiosity. I felt embarrassed, but then she shrugged and smiled and went back to eating in her dainty way. Her name might make her out to be a big or strong woman, but she is of medium build and called 'Mama' because of her age. She is nearly 75, but looks as if she might be in her early 50s. That night I went to bed pleased and thrilled and overwhelmed. I felt a tug in my heart, though, to leave *Casa Brillante*. I felt God talking to me, telling me to leave, that I had gotten myself into deep trouble. But I disregarded the feeling as being the result of my common fear of difference and change. In that oversize feather-bed with its comforting canopy and curtains, I soon fell into an exquisite sleep from which I awoke the following morning at dawn as refreshed as I had ever felt before. As I floated down to breakfast, I was greeted by five new faces intermingled with others more familiar. Emilia was serving the food to everyone seated while Cordon was now playing the cello. Henri, the handyman, was seated with the new friends who I guessed had just arrived, or maybe had come sometime in the night. A medium-height man sat at one end of the table while Mama Tilo sat at the other.

'Good morning, Aaron. I would like for you to meet our friends who have come to visit. Everyone, this is our guest of honor Aaron Sunderland.'

'I noticed that Delia and Celia were seated with everyone else. I thought this to be odd, but after all, it was the liberated early 80s, so good for them, right?

The Teachings of Don Luan

'Aaron, at the head of the table is our dear friend and
cohort in crime Arlo Costanada, author of a few books you
may be familiar with. To his left is Millaya Johnson, then
Kiki Willow, Regario Nostrali, and La Mora. And I believe
you have already met Goliath, Mr. Grey, Mr. Avelar, Celia
Durante, Delia Minchin, and Emilia Blodmonath.'

'Each man stood as he was introduced, and bowed to me.
The women each turned to me and made me feel welcome
with smiles and friendly eye contact. Goliath came over and
nudged my knee. Anyway, breakfast with my new friends was
delectable. Sliced apples, espresso, ham and cheese börek,
and a real surprise called *tromp l'oeil*, a dessert masterfully
designed to look like soft-boiled eggs and toast, and
apparently named after the art style. I wondered who the
chef was. After we ate, the day—and my new life—shot off to
a quick start. Mama Tilo took me into the gardens where we
were joined by Kiki Willow, Millaya Johnson, La Mora,
Delia, Emilia, and Celia—eight women sitting around in
comfortable wicker chairs with Goliath relaxing lazily at our
feet and snapping at butterflies who flitted around his head
as if he were a garden of flowers himself. I was soon
informed matter-of-factly that there are two kinds of
sorcerers—*dreamers* and *stalkers*—and that I was a mixture
of both, by my spiritual configuration. I was, they said, a
somnambulita, and they would like to begin calling me
Ensueña instead of Aaron, if I didn't mind. The name fit me
much better, they said, than an outdated male name from an
even more outdated religion. Though at first I winced at their
outright attack on Judeo-Christianity, I felt totally accepted
for the first time in my life, I'm sad to report, so I soon
readily agreed with everything they said, putting all of my
psychological training on the back burner, and forgetting
about my Christian upbringing altogether. In a big way, they
didn't trap me, I trapped myself. They wanted something
from me, a completion of what they were—and that
something, after half a decade, I have stolen back from them.
And I know that they are like mad hornets now, because I
have destroyed their all-important pattern of 8 women and 5
men. Sorcerers separate into smaller praxis groups of two or
three. So, there are no longer 13 of them, a magic number
traditionally used by groups of initiates the world over, good
and evil. Jesus had 12 apostles, making 13 of them. I, a
dreamer-stalker or *somnambulita*, was the third woman to
join La Mora, a *stalker*, and Mama Tilo, a *dreamer*. But I'm

tired, so you'll need to read Arlo's books if you want to know more.'

'Oh, I've read all of them—several times each,' replied Don as he stood and moved to his door. 'Thank you so much for telling us your story, Aaron. I can see that you're tired, though. Goodnight, and see you very soon.'

I stood to leave with Aaron.

'I need to be alone with God right now, Bastion, if you don't mind.'

'Me? Mind?' I felt elated, encouraged. 'Go on and do yo thang, mama!' Then I felt like an idiot. I was a social retard when I was younger—something in the Pensacola air, I guess—but the residuals still blurted out of my dumbass mouth on occasion. When Aaron chuckled, though, I felt relieved.

'Goodnight, Bastion. See you tomorrow. It's my move-in day, remember?'

'I didn't forget.' My face felt hot. 'Nighty-night, sweetheart.'

Her eyes widened and lips parted in surprise. 'Oh Bastion! You called me *sweetheart*!' She ran and threw her arms around me.

Now I was beet red, and stayed that way until I fell asleep, but not until after O'Neill got all the details about the 'smokin' blonde' he saw me with. All the details I cared to tell him, anyway—which amounted to about one sentence. 'She's my friend.'

A sacred union begins with trustful privacy.

24

La Mora

This is the part of the story that I am most sad to tell about. Why? Because the most terrible thing ever for any lover is the fact that he hasn't spent enough time with his Beloved when he could have—and that there was nothing more important in the world, in *any* world.

After I had completely disregarded my promise to Aaron, and after La Mora and I had enjoyed for several hours great conversation about the mystique of Hollywood over rich black coffee, shortbread, and a delicious drink made of milk and coconut sugar that has been introduced to a quantity which makes the concoction taste exactly like chocolate, this wily 'spider-woman,' ever soft-spoken and ladylike, stood from her chair and knelt before me on the red oval carpet which had been thrown in front of the enormous hearth in the main room of her Beverly Hills mansion.

'I want to show you something, Bastion,' she whispered as she closed her eyes.

I was wildly entranced, not only by her stunning beauty— her dark shining eyes, her thick auburn hair, her toned and tanned petite physique—but by her house itself. It was a Spanish style mansion built in the latter part of the 19th Century, a far cry from the decrepit yet lovable Regency I had grown to adore, or any other antiquated building situated on the nasty, stinking, littered streets of a usually rainless, smoggy[1] Hollywood.

The room we were in was more than king-size, it was phenomenal. Its walls were painted white, and the solid oak rafters in the cathedral ceiling had been treated in such a way that they revealed all of their natural beauty. The floor was made of glazed cerulean tile. Earlier, on a whim while La Mora was still in the kitchen somewhere far away preparing our food and drink, I ran my fingers over several places— across the tile in a few prime areas, in corners, over main walking areas, beside the baseboards and on the chair rails,

---

[1] The word 'smog' is a blend of the words 'smoke' and 'fog' and was coined by French scientist Dr. Des Voeux at a July 3, 1905, Public Health Council meeting in London.

beneath tables and couches, across window seats and under chairs. To my astonishment, I found not one speck of dust, not one insect carcass or even gossamer wing, no hidden cobwebs—no debris of any kind whatsoever. *Nothing.* Was I impressed? *Flabbergasted* would be a better word. Not even the most precise and highly-paid maid—or team of maids—could do the job I discovered had been done there. It was simply an impossible task. There would be a speck of something, a dot of dust or a crumb in the shadows. But no. *Nothing.*

I sat nearly dumbfounded in the chair La Mora had offered me. I felt a nagging inside which I knew told me that I was approaching this meeting all wrong, but I was enamored by this stunning, beguiling witch—and that's never a good thing for an avowed witch-hunter.

La Mora spoke with her eyes still closed. 'Are you quite sure, Bastion, that you want to destroy me and my lineage? That you want to lead me to your God, as you have said, and show me that it is only him who deserves our praise? Wouldn't it be easier to take the higher road and just love everybody, let people do their own thing? Isn't that what Jesus teaches? Love everybody?'

I sat there smiling like a village idiot. Unexpectedly throwing everything that I knew was right to the Santa Ana Winds, I longed with every fiber of my being to lose my virginity to this woman, and this woman alone. I wanted to be her man, her plaything if she so desired. Wouldn't she be the perfect teacher for me? Wouldn't she be gentle and patient, fun and alive, erotic and deeply pleasurable? I wasn't a bad catch myself—good genes, strong, athletic, responsible, creative, witty, energetic. I had been offered love by a plethora of really cute girls since I had arrived in Hollywood—the kind most men scrape raw their bottom lips over—but in these moments of desire with La Mora I convinced myself that none of them did it for me. Not one, I now believed—not even Aaron—represented what I had always hoped for. But La Mora—yes, now *she* was perfect! And it seemed that she was submitting herself to me as she knelt there in front of me. I was young, and even younger at heart, but I had learned to read body language and tone of voice, and if I wasn't mistaken, this woman wanted me—right then and right there. What was my biggest clue? She stood, let her dress drop to the floor, knelt again, spread her knees apart, and began to caress herself.

The Teachings of Don Luan

I had it all planned out in that stupid mid-twenties head of mine. I'd work my way up from bookseller to somewhere good in Hollywood. I had my eye on being a writer there. *Yes.* That's what I would do. I'd reevaluate my assumed reason for being in L.A.—the girl Jennifer—and turn to embrace this sort of 'witchcraft,' because La Mora was not old and bony and mean-spirited, and she certainly didn't have green skin and a hairy pink wart on the tip of her nose. There was a besom[1] by her fireplace, but it looked more like decoration than a mode of hellish drug-induced travel on Walpurgis Night. Yes, that's what I would do. I would embrace this *brujería* not as the witchcraft it was purported to be, not as the sorcery that Aaron had apparently stupidly left for some reason, but as the perfect Southwestern expression of freedom and love, just as Costanada and the others insisted that it was. Why, after all, should I disbelieve him? Wasn't that the whole point of my Christianity— freedom and love? The word 'Nonfiction' was right there on the spine of every book Costanada wrote. So, I'd give myself—head, hands, feet, and everything in between—to La Mora, and then I would study all of Costanada's books and really get to know him and the other sorcerers in their 'lineage,' and all would be well. I'd probably even get to meet all of them and maybe even actually join them, and then bring my own Christian beliefs into play with their own— maybe I would even then go back and revolutionize the Church itself with teachings apparently lost through the hundreds and hundreds of years! Surely these amazing sorcerers would accept my thoughts, and accept me. And surely God would accept these people as the *other* sheep in his fold.

It was settled. I would become La Mora's love slave.

Abruptly, a striking figure appeared behind the kneeling, massaging object of my arduous desire. It was a man. He was dressed in a coat made of coarse animal hair. He wore a wide belt of leather around his waist. He also carried a hefty staff of oak or some other hardwood. His locks were long but pulled back to reveal a full, unruly beard that hung past his belt. His obsidian eyes were not kind. They blazed with an inner inferno. He raised his staff with both hands and, without any hesitation in his movement, swung it at La

---

[1] A handmade broom used in witchcraft ceremonies.

Mora. As it flew toward her, it became a scimitar, yet the blade passed through her neck as if the imposing man and his weapon were mere ghosts. I knew, though, that he was far more than a spectral impression. La Mora jolted as if she had actually been beheaded. Her eyes popped open and bulged in abject terror. She reached for me, her lips mouthing words I couldn't hear or understand, her expression begging me for protection. She tried to stand, but couldn't for some reason. Then, quite suddenly, she seemed to be calmed by something. She took several deep breaths and closed her eyes again. I swooned, then sat up in my chair, but for some reason I couldn't stand up either. The rustic man was still behind La Mora, his eyes yet filled with fury. I felt cold, and then hot, and then cold again. I felt sad, and horrified, and grieved in my spirit. I began to weep. La Mora moved to all fours and began to sway her head from side to side, and then up and down. Her eyes now open, she looked up and stared at me impassively, almost as if I wasn't even there, as if she were gazing right through me. I felt repulsed. I stood up to leave, but the powerful man held up his left palm to me as if to say 'Stop—move no further.' I sat back down, aghast and sweating even though, according to the pretty brass wall thermometer, the temperature in the house was a perfect 70 degrees.

La Mora began to sing. At first her song sounded off-tune, but then I realized it was some kind of chant, maybe one from some ancient culture she had studied. I had never heard the song before, or anything like it. She maintained her disinterest in me. Then I noticed a change in her. At first it was slight. Her hair began to lengthen, half inch by half inch, and then her perky, celestial nose began to widen until it reached an inhuman width, the nostrils broadening far beyond anything functional, and then adding a third opening for good measure. Then, as if I watched a film sped up from days to seconds, hair began to grow from her face in quick spurts—but not her face only, all over her body in thick tufts so that in no more than a minute or two she was covered in long, silky reddish hair—*that bled*. Then, when she yawned and stared at me with hatred, I blacked out for a second. Long, pointed yellow fangs do that to me. Was she simian, or even similar to simian? *No.* She was unearthly, and maybe hellish, because from her forehead now protruded five three-inch spikes, horns maybe, but they glowed with a greenish metallic sheen. More hair that bled grew all over her so that she was soon a massive blood-soaked hirsute ball, for lack of a better explanation. I say 'ball' because she began to roll and bounce around the room and then back toward me at an alarming rate, blood flying everywhere. I screamed like a little girl, jumped from my chair so fast my head spun like Linda Blair (who I actually met once on Melrose Ave.), and vaulted across the spacious parlor to the safety of, yes, *a locked door*. I turned, terrified, and looked for the stranger who had clearly come to break La Mora's spell over me and alter my perception, but he was no longer there, or at least no longer visible to me. When it dawned on me who he was, deep shame added itself to the sheer panic I felt as I was being chased around this once-immaculate room by a rolling ball of filthy, growling, gory, snorting hair. *The Blood-Slinging Hair Monster*. No, that sounds too much like a quirky 'B' Horror flick. How about *I Was A 20-Something Dumb Ass*. There. That's better. The delightful little Hollywood classic 'Ding! Dong! The Witch Is Dead!' began to play in my head as I leaped over and dodged couch after ottoman after end-table after flamboyant flower vase. Finally, I located the front door of her mansion, and I found myself grateful beyond words that we weren't somewhere out in the boondocks of Sonora. To my pleasant surprise, I found that Doc Martens work great as running shoes, but a 600 mile trek back to my pad in Hollywood would have been pretty taxing, even for a young buck like myself able to race the city bus on my mountain bike down Beverly Boulevard—and win.

I flew all the way home to the Regency—about 3 miles, give or take. But I knew it wasn't over, not by a long shot. After all, La Mora still had another place to live not far from me at all. Three doors down on the same side, as I remembered.

Don't say it. I know how stupid I am. Aaron Sunderland—the girl of my dreams—a renewed disciple of Jesus and also my girlfriend, and I go and do *this* idiocy? Well, the bright side is that every last shred of self-righteousness that had been embedded in me as a Southern Baptist boy back in good old P'cola, Florida was burned out of me the night I was sprinkled the demoniac blood of La Mora. I really needed to spend some time with Don. And Aaron. And God. This situation we were in wasn't bad. *It was way bad.*

When I got home, I took a long, hot shower and then, after sleeping for a few hours, woke up wide awake only to 'drive the porcelain bus' until dawn. When I woke up at 10 the next morning, I was super glad it was my day off from work. Later I had a taco salad at a place not a far walk from my house. I rationalized that maybe Bob would let me slide a few days into the following month's rent. Gotta live a little, right?

25

Rub-a-Dub-Dub,
Three Girls in a Tub

I was on my way east on Beverly Boulevard—the sane street in Hollywood—when I had a flat tire. The Spokes-n-Things bike shop owner had sold me a lemon, and then every time I walked my bike in to have it fixed (which usually took me several hours from the breakdown point) he would say 'Go a little easier on her.' *Easy?* In Hollywood dodging city buses, BMWs, and Saabs like nobody's business? In the bigger picture, my sky-blue mountain bike was the one I needed for the time I lived in Hollywood, but a little more honesty and morals from the businessman would have been welcomed. So anyway, I was on my way down Beverly Blvd., just past Martel Ave. when, yep, I ran over something in the road that punctured my tire. So I'm standing there on the sidewalk now. It's nearly 4:30 in the afternoon, I've been at work since 7:30, and the bike shop closes at 6. Not a big deal. All I have to do is to push my bike through the desert wintry winds back to the bike shop. Anyway, so I'm about to start my mile or so trek when a car pulls up behind me. Now at any hour of the day in Los Angeles when a car pulls up behind you and doesn't shut its engine off, you have reason to believe that you could be enjoying your last few seconds on Earth. But, as it stood, I had 15 minutes of sunlight left, and so, yes, like the old song goes, while California dreamin' on such a winter's day, I began to pray, and would have even walked into a church had there been one available.

'Hey good-lookin'!'

Moi? I turned. Three foxy girls were hanging out of their silver BMW in various provocative ways, all beckoning to me, all saying things like 'C'mere, beautiful!' and 'Need a ride?' and 'Yeah baby!' and 'Woo-hoo!' I'll admit that this gave my formerly socially awkward flesh a much-needed boost. Not that I needed such a boost now that I had been honored with a shocking blonde model type as my dedicated, loving, God-fearing girlfriend, but men are naturally dogs no matter how you slice us. It's not anything to ever be proud of after the fact, and in this particular instance all I can say is that I had grace upon grace upon grace upon grace poured all over me in far more volume than the one or two lumps of sugar Def

Leppard was offering to pour over everybody—well, mainly their girl fanbase—within MTV viewing range at that time. That said—

'Get in, hot boy!'

I stupidly got in after they hooked my bike onto their rack in the back. A BMW for girls gone wild, years before 'Girls Gone Wild.'

'Where are we going?'

'Where you headin', baby?'

'Bike shop up on Melrose.'

'Then that's where we're goin'.'

We dropped my bike off. The owner said I could pick it up the next morning by 9. Then he added that maybe I should go a little easier on her. Well, I had to be at work at 8, so that meant I would have to take the bus down La Brea to Beverly and then out to the Beverly Center where I worked. No big deal, because I had ridden the bus before, but I doubted a trip to Beverly Hills would be anywhere near as adventuresome as the time I got lost in Inglewood on my way to Venice, or the time I got lost in Venice on my way back to Hollywood. If you know those areas, either good for you or bad for you, depending. If you don't know what I'm talking about, pray you never do. But, there *are* things worse than getting lost in one of the most dangerous cities on the planet. Let me explain.

We dropped my bike off, as I said, and the three cuties offered me a ride home. I liked them and trusted them, but on the way they suggested we hang for a bit in their hot-tub and then after that go up to Griffith Observatory and look out over Los Angeles and take in all its millions of spectacular lights. I had done that once or twice, and since there is hardly anything more beautiful to do at night in L.A., slaphappy me agreed to go with them, and off we sped. On the way, we did the full introduction thing, them saying their names were Claudia, Dori, and Emma. I'm sure by now you've guessed who the three girls *really* were. You got it: Celia, Delia, and Emilia. I had no idea, of course, that my party girls were the Three Witches. I knew that such women existed because Costanada had mentioned them and then Aaron had told me and Don about them, but what were the chances that three giddy girls in a BMW would locate me on an obscure section of Beverly Blvd. minutes after I had a flat tire on my bike? Well, since there are no such things as coincidences, and chances therefore also go out the window like ghost-birds on the breeze, I fell into yet another part of the plan for my life—and theirs—and became captive to three malicious sorcerers who masqueraded as whoop-it-up merrymakers. Apparently my one major weakness was known by the infernal powers that be, but I was protected after all, because there exist other powers a bit stronger and with a far broader scope than tempting spirits who like to possess barefoot reprobate desert rats dressed in skimpy halter tops and thigh-high skirts. Still, all three of them were cute as buttons, and that was my initial downfall.

After the hot-tub experience at a mansion in the 2200 block of Vista Del Mar and me somehow maintaining my innocence despite groping fingers, flicking pink tongues, and hungry eyes, we drove the nearly 4 miles up to Griffith Observatory. The sun had fully set by then, and, indeed, the City showed herself below us with all of her radiant magnificence. I saw her hair was burning, her hills were filled with fire. If I said I never loved her, you know I'd be a liar. I guess Jim Morrison will always be a favorite poet of mine, sad wad of angst that he was. A lot like me, actually.

Emilia approached me with all of her willowy suave. 'Wanna see something, Bastion?'

I nodded, hoping it wouldn't be her naked pudendum thrust into my face like some kind of hot-from-the-oven pot pie. Yes, that had happened before. No, I had not partaken, and it wasn't my plan to partake this time either. I had gotten this far. I could wait for Aaron on our wedding night.

As if it was the most natural act in the world, Emilia took a deep breath and then lifted off the ground in front of me. She rose to about 15 feet. All three girls began to laugh as if they enjoyed an inside joke together. I wasn't laughing, or even chuckling. I knew what I had gotten myself into, and I knew I wouldn't be able to get myself out of it. Somebody else would have to do that. 'Jesus,' I whispered. Emilia fell to her knees like a Raggedy Ann doll let go by a three-year-old who's seen something more fun to do than play house.

No matter what godless agenda a person carries, whether it's witchcraft for the control of a few or perverted 'rights' that adversely affect the masses who believe traditionally and historically about marital status and familial values, the actions and words are always the same when it all gets down to brass tacks.

Emilia screwed up her face with the pain from her fall. 'Jesus Christ! That fuckin' *hurt*, ya Bible-thumpin' jagoff!'

Jagoff. Huh. Who would have thought? Emilia was from Pittsburgh. How funny. 'How 'bout them Steelers?' I replied. She did not laugh. I looked up from where she sat on the ground rubbing her bruising knees to see Celia and Delia circling and snickering with each other like two little girls at play—two little girls at play twenty feet off the ground whose heads were now twice as big as their bodies and whose feet were ribbons of smoke that trailed behind them like kite tails. Before I grayed out and then lost consciousness, I remembered the bitter cola the girls had offered me in the car. For years I had been a fan of bitter colas like *Moxie* and one or two others—even if I had to make them myself. Delia had unscrewed the cap on the bottle they gave me, and I had assumed, since I liked the girls, that they were cool. Never assume.

Drugs do wondrous things to the mind—especially drugs that have been concocted for sensory heightening and mind alteration.[1] Whatever the Three Witches gave me in my drink, it was some kind of 'zombie drug,' and that's exactly how I felt when they told me to get back in their car, that they were going to take me somewhere really nice. I adored their strange new words *'nice'* and *'really'* and *'car,'* so, laughing like a hyena, I happily complied and lay down in the back seat across the laps of Delia and Celia. A furious Emilia put the petal to the metal and flew across the mountain like nobody's business. I, though, felt as if I was lying back in my grandmother's swing in South Flomaton, Florida. Celia and Delia said a few things like 'careful!' and 'watch yourself!' I loved these words more than 'nice,' 'really,' and 'car,' whose syllables smelled like honeysuckle, whereas the words of warning to Emilia smelled like cut grass—not an altogether bad scent, but one that's far more common, especially in the warmer months.

The girls took me up to the world-renowned 'Hollywood Sign' and let me out. They said they'd be back in a few minutes to get me. Well, if you know anything about that part of Mount Hollywood, you know it's wild. Not much up

---

[1] φαρμακεία (*pharmakeía* from *pharmakeuō*, 'administer drugs') – properly, drug-related sorcery, like the practice of magical arts, *etc*. We derive the English words *pharmacy* and *pharmaceuticals* from this word. Interestingly enough, the Irish for *witch* is *medicine*.

there, really. Except ravenous coyotes who rove in packs,[1] hungry bear, and maybe the odd mountain lion or two who are especially noted for their empty bellies and a no-holds-barred approach to food gathering. Nothing too spine-tingling.

Well, wouldn't you know it? Not long after the witch-car swirled away in a cloud of magical mountain dust, I was surrounded by five snarling coyotes, and not an armed security guard or even an old man with a walking stick anywhere in sight. Why would these nice animals be up at the 'Hollywood Sign' on a cold and getting colder night anyway? Shouldn't they be hunkered down in their cave somewhere, or maybe a hole or whatever ravenous wild canines live in? I backed myself up against what I thought might be the backside of the giant 'Y' and stood there with my eyes closed, praying and suddenly a lot more sober than I had been a minute before. Growls and snarls are not the most fun things to hear at any time, but when they are intended to make a victim panic into submitting to their owners' bloodthirsty, crouching, circling wishes at the moment, they're a bit worse than when, say, your father is

---

[1] It is believed that more than 5,000 coyotes roam the City of Los Angeles. Thousands more live throughout the county. Mostly, these animals live in foothills in and around the city. Coyotes are highly intelligent, adaptable, and possess excellent sensory abilities. Urbanized coyotes can survive on a variety of foods including garbage, feeding by people, food left out for pets, and small pets themselves. Zoos have had to deal with these predators feeding on zoo exhibits. Coyotes are adaptable predators, tolerant of human activities, and quick to adapt and adjust to changes in their environment. They are likely to lose natural aversion to people when competition among coyotes increases for sources of food. The biggest problems occur when people feed coyotes - either wittingly or unwittingly. Coyote attacks, when they occur, are commonly directed against small animals and pets. Although it is very rare, coyotes have attacked humans. There were 37 reported attacks on humans in Los Angeles County between 1978 and 2003, including an August 1981 attack in Glendale on a 3-yr-old girl proving fatal because of massive bleeding and a broken neck.

irate with your mother for keeping a devastating secret he has now discovered, or when your mother is infuriated with the neighbor lady who has threatened to spank you just for being a rambunctious kid. I had a pretty interesting childhood—in the Chinese sense of the word 'interesting.' You know, *May you live in interesting times* and all that. Come to think of it, I've never gotten that saying in any fortune cookie I've ever snapped opened. I don't wonder why, really. A proper understanding of it could ruin a fine meal of Cashew Chicken and *sashimi*.

I opened my eyes, spoke the Name I love, and in a New York minute, as the old song goes, all five coyotes turned tail, yelped like they had bitten down on a live electric wire, and raced away into the Hollywood underbrush. That was the first of my difficulties taken care of, and, yes, I was grateful. The next leg of my trial was to navigate the several miles back down the mountain to the Regency and my creaky, springy, uncomfortable Murphy bed.[1] Thankfully my navigation took me through lots of ultra-wealthy suburban neighborhoods. Well, I say *thankfully*, but what else are police officers going to do with themselves at 9 PM on a mellow, freezing Monday night? Thank goodness I was still dressed for work, my necktie a little askew but still around my neck. That and my clean-cut look relative to the usual code of dress in Hollywood at the time are likely the two main elements that saved my neck. Well, and the heavily

---

[1] William L. Murphy was a bachelor living in a cramped studio apartment in San Francisco in 1884. At the time, it was not socially acceptable for single men to socialize with women in a room with a bed. Since Murphy had to constantly maneuver around the furniture when entertaining, he decided to design a bed that could rest against the wall when it wasn't in use. He began experimenting with a folding bed, pivoted on the doorjamb of a dressing closet and then lowered into its standard position. By the early 1900s, Murphy's idea was patented and the Murphy Bed was in production. Murphy Bed sales rapidly increased as city life gained popularity and space was at a premium. The Murphy Bed Door Company moved its headquarters to New York City in 1925. During its heyday, the company produced more than 50,000 Murphy Beds annually.

armed guardian angel I caught out of the corner of my eye. Scared? I was petrified. Filled with fresh anti-witchcraft vengeance? You betcha. That said, part of me reminded myself that the more one stirs a pile of shit, the worse it stinks. But the overpowering part of me convinced myself that this same pile of shit eventually hits the fan, or becomes a creek upon which one often finds himself without a paddle, so it's best to deal with said shit accordingly before things get out of hand. Prayer starts due process, and sometimes ends everything right there—if we trust enough, that is.

I don't remember going to sleep, or even getting home safely, but both apparently happened, and in a few hours I awoke if not refreshed then certainly thankful to be alive.

In my nightmares he's been stalking me for the past six months, or year—maybe longer. I hear his footsteps behind me. I stop. He stops. The city holds its breath. The wind drops a newspaper from its clenched fist. Pages skitter across the sidewalk like unhappy rats. I walk again. He fills a void behind me. We pass a beat cop. I say not a word. This threat can't be classified, much less reported. Crowds of theater-goers are useless. They only know drama when it's staged. I glimpse into store windows as I hurry by. Each one offers a little of me, a suggestion of him. There's nothing clear. A curl of cigarette smoke, the outline of a face, a posture. I try to outdistance him. But where am I going anyhow? What if *he's* the end of my journey? I run for a few blocks, past the bank, the fire station, the breakfast dive, the seedy bar, all the places shut up tight. He doesn't run. He rides my draft until his breath flutters the hairs of my neck. I want to scream 'What do you want with me!' But what if *that's* what he wants with me? *My terror.*

26

Cordon

'You're going *where*?' Aaron's voice was three pitches higher than usual.

'To *Casa Brillante*.'

'Look, I forgive you for what happened with La Mora. The same thing happened to me years ago, or something similar anyway. I can see—I mean, I know what she is capable of, what kind of power she can conjure over people, men and women alike. She even likes to tell people that her ancestors hail from the Isle of Lesbos.'

'I'm ashamed, and angry.'

'Angry is fine. You'll need anger. But don't be ashamed. You've confessed, you're forgiven, and cleansed. That's what the Blood does for us—the Heart Womb of Jesus. It sets us free to live, to act, and to truly love. And to truly go to war, against the unseen enemy, in that love. But, you're serious? *Casa Brillante*. Can't you just show up at CG & Co. in Westwood and do whatever it is God is telling you to do there? Why go all the way out into the Mojave Desert, so far away from help if you should need it? Who will help you then? I mean, I'm confused. Is God telling you to do this, Bastion? Is *God* telling you to do this? Because if he isn't, may God help you.'

'He is telling me to go, and he's saying something else, but I want you to hear him too.'

'I'm going with you, aren't I.'

'So you heard him! *Yes*! I have two days off in a row next week, which is way out of the ordinary. Can we use your Saab?'

♪

We never know when we're going to die. The younger we are, the less we think about it. We may get sick, but we always believe we will recover. A special understanding, though, had been given to me at a young age. I was aware of my death, or the potential of it, and I felt ready to meet God because of my trust in his transformational power through his shed Blood—through my reconnective communion with his Presence. *The life of the flesh is in the blood* pretty much sums up the idea that the flesh avails nothing, but that it's the Spirit which gives life. Unusual, I know, and so very foreign to our own day's understanding of the world—to the point of sounding Medieval and, yes, insane. The saddest part of it all is that there are so many people who are outright threatened by Christian convictions. Why? Their own beliefs don't threaten me. But the minute I talk about God, they get riled up, as if—*yep*—as if my words actually hurt them. Quantum Mechanics proves that words do hurt after all, and the more a person is addicted to whatever mollifies his burning soul that needs only God, the more words of love for him are going to hurt him. So be it. I declared then, and I declare now, that I will walk, speak, and act in righteousness until God takes me home. If I'm wrong, I'll live a life of peacefulness and then sleep or disappear into the vast primordial soup—no sweat, no loss. But what if I'm right, and there *is* eternal life after death? Are people ready? Being good doesn't get it, by the way. A man dying of a poisonous snake bite can be good to those around him. He will still die unless the poison is drained from his veins in time. The Cross and the Blood does just that, there is no other cure known to man, and Jesus is the 'bronze serpent' that hangs there for us all. Pretty powerful arsenal, eh? Aaron thought so, so she got quiet in herself and discovered that God indeed was telling her to come with me. When my days off from work finally rolled around, we rode out into the sunrise.

♪

I want to give an even better idea of who I am, and who exactly was going up against this *brujería* coven. There's only one way to do this, in my estimation, and that is to tell a story about my childhood—you know, the *formative years*. I have a plethora of tales I could relate, but one in particular may provide some necessary information about my development, and maybe a few laughs to boot.

Ferry Pass Middle School, in Pensacola, Florida, would have won the prize for 'Most Bizarre School of the 1970s' had there been such a contest. The kids who attended there were brought in from two different elementary schools—Ferry Pass Elementary and Scenic Heights Elementary, each one about a mile away from the other. The first was populated with hundreds of poor kids and a handful of suburban kids all living on the north side of Olive Road, the second populated only with middle-class suburban kids all living south of Olive. But this difference in demographic doesn't seem to have mattered much. The suburban kids were as mean as the poor kids if they wanted to be mean, and sometimes even meaner. But to set 'mean' aside for a focus on 'bizarre,' let's introduce two of the surplus of Middle Schoolers at Ferry Pass: myself as a rotund, quiet 5'1' 7th grader, and the much taller 8th grader Porsche Wicksmith.

Porsche wore a hoodie—long before hoodies were even invented. Summer, Winter, Spring, Autumn—it didn't seem to matter. She always had her bluish-grey hood pulled over her long, greasy blondish hair, most likely in an attempt to hide her red-rimmed half-closed eyes. I'd be going to class and she'd be there, gazing down at me like some kind of gaunt giantess. A creepy grin always played around her thin blue lips as her elongated nose bumped the top of my head every time she coughed, which was a lot.

'Smoke a doobie? Hey, kid. Smoke a doobie with me?'

'No thank you,' I'd reply, terrified. Smoke a *what*? Oh, God! Does she mean *marijuana*? She does! *She means marijuana!*

'Smoke a doobie? *Ha-ha-ha!* Smek a doob? *Ha-ha-ha-ha-ha!*'

I would see Porsche every day, around every corner. Well, that's not *exactly* true. When I wasn't being taunted by this continually-stoned stick of a girl, there was the nameless little backwoods monstrosity with the long, greasy blondish hair who wore faded Levi bell-bottoms, worn-out suede wallabies (they were really cheap in the 70s), and a Hawaiian print polyester 'silk' shirt tucked in and unbuttoned to the belt, its sleeves rolled up over biceps smaller than the forearms preceding them.

'Hey man. Wanna buy a Now-or-Later?'

'No thanks,' I'd reply, jumpy and ready to scream.

'First one's free.'

I'd shake my head and walk away. He'd shrug his skinny shoulders and move on to the next kid—girl or boy—he thought might have money. 'Wanna buy a Now-or-Later? First one's free.' *Dang it!* Denied again. He would snitch several packs at the Majik Market convenience store around the corner, and then sell each individually-wrapped piece of candy for a quarter. Or a dime if that's all you had. But with that dime you also had to give him an unused pencil, or no deal. Seems he was the campus champion pencil-fighter as well as budding drug dealer.

No more than three minutes later, across campus, I would round a corner heading toward class.

'Wanna buy a Now-or-Later?'

'No. I already said *no*.'

'Ya sure?'

After class he would be waiting. 'Wanna buy a Now-or-Later?'

Lunchroom. 'Wanna buy a Now-or-Later?'

Hallway. 'Wanna buy a Now-or-Later?'

Breezeway. 'Wanna buy a Now-or-Later?'

Between buildings. 'Wanna buy a Now-or-Later?'

P.E. 'Wanna buy a Now-or-Later?' And he wasn't even in my grade, much less in my Phys. Ed. class.

'No! I said no!'

'Ya sure? First one's free.'

On my way to the bus after school, he'd be there. 'Wanna buy a Now-or-Later?'

Off the bus in the morning. 'Wanna buy a Now-or-Later?' Did he *live* at the school? *Was he even real?* Maybe he was a ghost. Maybe he had died in one of the infamous apple-throwing fights at Ferry Pass Middle School. He was a little guy. I had a hard time imagining him able to defend himself from a whistling red apple missile if he made somebody mad. *Anybody.* Even physically powerless Porsche Wicksmith.

My mind was in a constant whirl.

'Wanna buy a Now-or-Later?'

'Smoke a doobie?'

'Smoke a Now-or-Later?'

'Wanna buy a doobie?'

'Now or doobie?'

'Doobalater?'

'No! No! Dear God in Heaven, no! Leave me alone! Please—leave me alone!'

But they wouldn't leave me alone. Nobody would. The poor kids picked on me. The suburban kids picked on me. Even the ones who had discovered the brand-new game called *Dungeons & Dragons* picked on me. How did *they* pick on me? Well, they found out that I liked Tolkien, and that I was a visual artist. So, when I brought my colored-pencil renditions of Tolkien's characters to school to show them, they made fun of me and, to taunt me further, told me that until I had read the *Silmarillion*, I would never understand the Fantasy genre, or even literature at large. These are 13-yr-old 8th graders, now, claiming to understand the *Silmarillion*. But 'A/V Boy'[1] dweebs weren't the worst of my troubles. Not by a long shot.

'Wanna buy a Now-or-Later?'

'*No, damn you to Hell!* I do *not* want to buy a Now-or-Later!'

Oh God. Now I had cursed somebody to Hell. Now I was going to Hell myself. What would it be like in Hell? My mind raced, horrified. *Oh, Lord, no!*

'Wanna buy a Now-or-Later?'

'Hey kid. Smoke a doobie?'

'*Nah-ha-ha-ha-ha-ha!* The *Silmarillion*! Ya hafta smoke the *Silmarillion*!

Smoke a Tolkie? Hey kid, smoke a Tolkie? *Ha-ha-ha-ha-ha!* Smoke it now or smoke it later, you still hafta smoke it!'

'Wanna smoke a Now-or-Doobie? Hey kid! *Ha-har-har-har-harrr!*'

I ran screaming, and I'm still running, but not screaming so much these days. Why? Not one of those kids followed me to Hollywood, where I finished growing up quite apart from their closed-in worlds. There on the 'Boulevard of Broken Dreams' I developed my own verve where sweet-and-sour candy pushers, backwoods pot-smokers, and sarcastic dice-throwing board gamers fear to dwell.

I finally read the *Silmarillion*. It holds far more depth than any 8th grader could possibly grasp, no matter how academically dorky or 'dungeon mastery' he might be. I also delved into the world of the lackadaisical pothead for a little while before I realized the lifestyle was as stupid as I had thought it was as a 7th grader. But I never acquired a taste for the sweet-and-sour candy.

'Wanna buy a Now-or-Later? Just a quarter. First one's free.'

♪

Me driving with my super careful approach to vehicular transportation, it took us several hours to get out into the part of the Mojave Desert where *Casa Brillante* was—or was supposed to be.

---

[1] Audio/Visual

Aaron looked up from her *Atlas*. 'Bastion, I know where I am, but the turnoff's not right, the rock formations are all wrong, even the sky looks different.'

'Maybe I made a wrong turn somewhere back there near Flustercock, or maybe Fumbuck.'

'No. I'm your navigator. You did exactly as I told you to do, and I have it all mapped out, right here. No, something's wrong.'

'*Brujería* at work, ya think? Yeah, probably.'

'They knew we were coming, so they've moved the *hacienda*.'

My heart leaped into my gullet. I calmly cleared my throat, found a hard shoulder on the side of the highway, pulled over, and turned the engine off. I yanked in a deep breath. I turned and looked at Aaron, incredulous. A laughing smile played around her full, rosy lips. Her azure eyes sparkled in the early morning sunshine.

'You're kidding, right girlie? I mean, who can magically move a house?'

'Look. I said not *everything* Arlo says in his books is true about the coven. I didn't say *some* of it doesn't happen. Bastion, they're powerful. But you should know that, right? Or did you think you were going after a troop of Campfire Girls?'

I had no words yet. I studied Aaron up and down. She closed her eyes. Her lips moved as if she was praying.

'So, you are actually telling me that Costanada and gang are powerful enough to relocate a mansion to wherever they would like it to be?'

'That's what I'm saying. I've seen them do it before. The same house was once on the Mexican side of the Sonoran Desert, a few miles outside Magdalena. Another time, it was near Assisi.'

'*Wait*. Assisi, Italy?'

'Yes, the one in Italy. And today it was supposed to be just outside Zzyzx, but as you can see, it isn't.'

'I'm having a problem trusting you right now, Aaron, as you might imagine, so I think I'll just turn around, drive back to Hollywood, speak to Bob our friendly apartment manager, and have your little *derrière* thrown out of the building!'

Aaron began to cry. I said I was sorry and tried to touch her hand. She pulled away and looked out the car window. Her shoulders shook for a few minutes. I felt like a heel. I said I was sorry again. She turned to me. Her eyes were filled with love and understanding.

'I know what the old nature inside a person can say and do when it's frightened, Bastion. You know I do. But I'm your friend. I am not a witch anymore, and I don't plan to kill you while only pretending to be the girl you are courting. I am *really* courting you, I *really* love you, and—' She turned pink with her next words that nearly slipped out. I knew what they were. I took her hand.

'I'm sorry, Aaron. I didn't mean any of it. This has been hard. But how can I clean Los Angeles of a coven of witches when I can't even control that mean little bastard inside of me?'

'You can't.'

I waited, unclear in my mind, puzzled.

'You can't, Bastion. No man or woman of God has ever been able to fight this world system by themselves, or even their own fleshly desires which, incidentally, keep that world system moving. That's the whole point of all this. You have been given the godly understanding to see that the world is poisoned through and through, and you've been given a deep love for others to keep that poison at bay, and given the fight to challenge practitioners of that poison who have become degenerate and unrepentant for their words and actions— and even their damaging thoughts. You are a prophet—like Nathan, like Elijah, like Elisha, like John the Baptist. But it is never by might nor by power, but only by the Spirit of God.'

My heart swelled and became full, and I cried like a baby for a long time as we sat there in the desert. How appropriate for a prophet. But I wasn't the first one who wept—and I wouldn't be the last.

♪

After Aaron and I had taken thirty minutes or so to quietly heal from our upset, I started the engine of her car.

'Where to now, Captain Bastion?'

'Well, my navigator, we drive blind until we find *Casa Brillante.*'

It was about seven in the morning now, still early. We had eaten a breakfast of sausage rolls and orange juice around 5:30, so neither one of us was hungry yet. We had coffee, and that did its number on me a few times during the trip, and on Aaron twice, but nobody was around, so restroom stops weren't necessary, if we could have even found them in the middle of the desert anyway. We had food for two weeks, extra clothes, freak snowstorm stuff if that should happen, a decked-out first aid kit complete with flares and orange safety vests and hats, plenty of money for gas and motel rooms if necessary, and guardian angels instead of the *Colt 38 Super* that Aaron used to carry while she placed full and unswerving trust in her magical powers.

I kept seeing a large house, Spanish style, in my mind. 'Aaron, I'm seeing a large house, Spanish style, in my mind.'

'What does it look like.'

'Large and Spanish style.'

She simpered. 'I mean the color scheme, gardens, doorways, roof, trees—things like that. Maybe people or animals? *Here*. Let me drive and you look again. In your mind, of course. It's large and Spanish style, by the way.'

I pulled over. It felt great to stretch my legs anyway. I really had to see a man about a horse, so, watching for Gila monsters and rattlesnakes, I trotted off into the underbrush so I could eventually think straight again. While I was negotiating a good price, I looked out over the vista spread before me, as a man will do when he's in the middle of a haggle, and what do I spy? A tiny white dot in the far-reaching distance—a white dot that could only be one thing. I strolled back to the car, dodging the odd tumbleweed, which I was terrified of as a little boy because I believed that if I ever saw one, it would also see me and chase me until it caught and ate me. I had somewhat of an overactive imagination back then.

When I got back to Aaron's Saab, apparently she was seeing a woman about a puppy, so I waited. When she got back, we switched seats as planned. She started the engine, it purred like a kitten, and we were *on the road again goin' places that we'd never been, seein' things that we may never see again.*

'Aaron, head up here and take the first road to your right—dirt, paved, it matters not.'

'Do what?'

'Please do as I suggest.'

'May I ask why?'

'Because I saw *Casa Brillante*.'

'You did? Where? When? *Oh—*'

'Yeah. You know. Back there. Anyway, as the crow flies, it's straight east of where we are right now. See? There's a road right there.'

She slowed and turned. It was unpaved and rocky. 'I'm going to have to drive really slow or I'll bottom out in a hole or something.'

'Drive like a turtle for all I care.' I looked over at the gas gauge. 'We still have more than plenty.'

Aaron nodded in agreement and let up off the pedal. 'She idles at about a mile and a half per hour without giving her gas, I think. I'll just hold the wheel and let her do her thing.'

'What's her idling RPM?'

'I wouldn't have a clue. I only half listened to my daddy when he was talking about cars. Oh, and I don't think turtles drive.'

♪

The going was slow and maddening. We were literally driving something like 3 or 4 miles an hour along a bumpy, potholed, rocky, sandy dirt road. A Mojave green, a kind of rattlesnake, slithered out in front of us at one interval, but it didn't seem threatened at all by our lumbering behemoth, so it took its happy time getting across the road and out into the sparse, hardy desert vegetation. I mused for a second and wanted to believe that, had I been bitten by it, or any other snake for that matter, I would have the necessary trust in God's will for my life to shake the animal off in the fire like St. Paul did on the Isle of Malta. I wanted to believe this, and now that I think about it again, that's one of the ways trust is built—by believing in the worldly impossible and making that impossibility null and void with a realer reality based solely in belief. I'm sure there's something 'quantum mechanical' about that idea, I just haven't done the research yet. In any case, it's nothing short of the magic children are so in love with. And, it's been written about for millennia. Witches put themselves through elaborate and expensive and often deadly rituals to get only a modicum of the power and peace available to the true Christian.

We kept driving. I got hungry and pulled out two ham sandwiches on rye. 'No mayo for you, right Aaron?'

'Thank you, Bastion. Yeah, I never liked mayonnaise.'

I tore into my sandwich like a starving pig.

'Wow, you're hungry!'

'Ju cood shay dat, jeah.'

'You should never talk with your mouth full. You could choke. Like Mama Cass did.'

I took a drink of water. 'That didn't actually happen, you know. And you should never take your eyes off the road! *Watch out!*'

We skidded to a halt just a few yards before we smashed into a massive twelve-foot log that was lying in the middle of the road.

Aaron took in a deep breath and then sighed as if she had just lain down a 50 pound pack. 'It's Cordon Grey.'

'Now, *who's* he again? Is he the gardener or the handyman?'

'He *plays* the gardener, and he's quite good at it because he actually loves plants. Anyway, he likes little tricks like this. I mean, look around. Do you see any giant trees anywhere that this log could have come from?'

I had to agree that hardwood forests in the Mojave were conspicuously absent. 'Well at least we know we're on the right track.'

'Yep, because they don't want us anywhere near their *hacienda*. Well too bad.' Aaron got out of the car and walked to the end of the log nearest her. My eyes must have bulged out on their stems, I don't know, but I felt alarm like I had never felt before when she squatted down, wrapped her arms around the massive tree, lifted it as easily as a child might lift a large pillow, pivoted in a wide semicircle away from the car, and deposited the tree onto my side of the road. Then she gave it a kick and made it roll down a slight incline obviously made by rainwater runoff, where it was soon stopped by bushes in the desert chaparral. I heard a frightened snake or other animal scurry away.

'How did you—'

'Like I said, it was Cordon Grey.'

'You said that, yes. But he must have used a crane or hoist or something to get it out here!'

'No, the tree itself.'

I went cold all over with terror. 'Wait just a flippin' minute! You— you mean to tell me, Aaron, that the tree trunk *itself* is Cordon Grey?'

'That's what I mean to tell you, yes.'

I wiped my suddenly sweaty brow. 'They're more powerful than I thought.'

'Yes. But, as you can see, we're even more powerful than they are.'

'*You're* more powerful! I'm just chopped lettuce on a paper plate. *Mommy*!'

'*Bastion*! You surprise me! Surely you haven't lost all your trust in this plan?'

'Where did that *Road Atlas* go? Oh here it is. Let's see now— I think we can be back for ice cream with Don by, let's say, noon?'

27

Goliath

I've called him 'Cujo' several times through the years. To my mind at the time, there was no difference. The cougar had made me nervous in the restaurant, but this time he scared the living daylights of out me. I'm pretty sure his ferocious roars and claw swipes at the Saab disturbed Aaron as well for the full ten minutes we both sat there in safety, though, unlike me, she didn't shriek like a baboon on fire. Simply put, Goliath would not let us out of the car without having Aaron and Bastion *tartare* for lunch. No blood was ever drawn, thankfully, but what blood *can* be drawn when it's pooled down around the ankles in sheer terror of pumping through the system for fear of being shed? No blood that I'm aware of.

So, did we find ourselves parked in the *hacienda* driveway where maybe somebody could have come out and talked to Goliath? You know, called him off the hunt? That's a laugh. We hadn't even driven two feet from where Aaron kicked Cordon Grey aside like a twig when Goliath was on us like white on rice. Where did the monstrous beast come from? It's anybody's guess.

'We can get past this too, Bastion. *Really.*'

I looked out at the gargantuan feline baring his fangs at me, growling and screaming as if, like Cujo, he had rabies. 'I'm open to all suggestions, Aaron. Barring gettin' out of this car. That's a definite Whisky á *No*-Go.'

'Goliath's human.'

'So I've been told, Aaron, but that piece of information doesn't makes things a thousand times scarier at all. No, I'm not too sure I have the owner's manual for that one.'

'I do.' Aaron took a deep breath, opened the car door, and stepped out, her pretty calf-length pink dress floating vaguely in the wintry breeze. I screamed and hid my face. In my mind I watched her torn into little shreds. I heard her wails of terror and pain—heard her prayers for mercy. I saw the wild-eyed, vicious cat tear into her flesh, disembowel her, drink her blood—

Goliath shot away from my side of the car, the window glass, now rolled up, serving as my only protection—which, by the way, I was sure he could easily bite through in order to get at my face and spine, if he really wanted to risk getting shards of glass in his mouth. Being a monster from the pit of Hell, I decided that he wouldn't have minded at all. When he saw Aaron standing there calm, cool, and collected, he halted, dropped to the dirt, and rolled over on his side for a tummy rub.

'C'mere, boy! *C'mon*!' Goliath looked at Aaron for a second as if he wasn't sure, but then he stood back up on all fours, moseyed over, nudged her with his nose, then licked her hand she held out for him—palm up like a smart person. 'That's a good boy, Goliath. The man in my car is my friend Bastion. Go say *hi*.'

I stiffened with apprehension. 'We have met, Aaron. I do not think that he liked me. In fact, I *know* he did not like me.' Goliath's teeth looked like vampire fangs. *Great.* A bloodsucking cougar who was actually a human sorcerer in disguise. 'What's he going to do next? *Fly*?' Well, I spoke to soon, I guess, because, as if on my suggestion, Goliath elevated several feet off the ground and hovered there for a second. Then he floated around to my side of the car again and put a paw up on the window, purring.

'Roll your window down, or just get out. He won't hurt you.'

'I have a better idea. Why don't *you* roll back into the driver's seat and then we'll we roll forward, do a little three-point turn around, and then get the guacamole out of Dodge! Sound good? I think I might even have a Ennio Morricone cassette on me somewhere for little background music to the scene. Does your cassette player work? Where's my cigar stub? I know it's around here somewhere—'

'Too funny! But seriously, get out and pet Goliath.'

'How does a person—assuming that's what I still am at this terrorized point—pet the hovering, salivating feline version of the most feared Philistine in history, pray tell? And I'm afraid I left my sling and stones back at the shepherd shack, stupid me.'

'You're just on a roll, aren't you! *Ha-ha!* Goliath! Float back a few feet and let Bastion get out. I mean *David*! Ha-ha!'

Goliath did as commanded, but I did not do as suggested.

'*Bastion*. How do you expect to tackle the rest of the sorcerers at *Casa Brillante* if you can't even handle a stick in the road and a big, lovable house-cat? Please get out and make friends. Look. I promise that if he bites you, I'll dress your wounds.'

'That's so comforting, Aaron. Do you know how to push intestines back in and bind them up, because that's precisely what you would need to know how to do. I hope you realize that, and also that you are in great danger of losing me here in the next few seconds or so. It was super nice knowing you, and unfortunately we never even made it to the Biblical version of that knowing. Mores the pity, but even if I should somehow survive this assault, I would no longer have a sword to be sheathed anyway. Certain things about a man have a tendency to shrivel permanently when they find themselves under extreme duress—or violently clawed out, whichever comes first.'

'Alright, alright! *Ha-ha!* You are *hilarious*, you know that? You're auditioning at the *Improv* when we get back to Hollywood! Anyway, Goliath won't bite or tear your guts or other parts out, will you Goliath? Bastion, give him a command to prove he can hear you and will do as you say.'

'Wait just a minute. You have already confirmed Arlo's statement that Goliath is human. Felines don't lie. They don't have the capacity to lie. Humans lie. All the time. You know that. I know that. And I'm sure the 'floating witch' Señor Goliath here knows that. No, I will not exit this vehicle until we are safely parked on North Orange Drive in front of the Regency—minus one humongous cougar. Game over. We're leaving now, Aaron, with or without you.'

'*We're* leaving with or without me? Looks like your trust has gone to the dogs.'

'I only *wish* there were some dogs here right now! And I never thought I'd say it, but those dogs could even be coyotes for all I care!'

Despite my witty retort, Aaron's words made me feel ashamed. She was right. What was I doing? Playing the victim again, and getting angry when things didn't go exactly my way. *Victimizing others when things didn't go exactly my way.*

Locating a strength that certainly was not mine and never had been, I opened the door and got out. I could not feel my feet or legs. I felt light. Maybe I was a ghost. Maybe Goliath had already ripped me into itty-bitty shreds. I took a deep, cool desert breath. Yep, my lungs were still working fine. Goliath drifted there in the air, still salivating like a hungry child in a chocolate shop. I tried not to visualize being eaten while still alive. The attempt somewhat worked. I escaped the hideous thought with nothing more than an imaginary chomp of my forearm that stung like the dickens. As I shook that infernal vision off, Goliath gazed at me and then wafted over like an enormous hairy butterfly. With teeth. You might not think it possible that a floating feline could knock a person down with as much force as one that might jump up on a person. Think again. There I lay with Goliath's front paws pressing down on my chest and rib cage. 'Aiiiiiuhh! Help!'

Goliath hopped off me and ran to Aaron. They both came back to where I was now sitting up, bewildered and really wanting a chili burger and some hot fries. You know, comfort food—for an uncomfortable situation. Aaron crawled into the car for a second and then brought me out a PBJ and a cold drink. 'Here. This'll make you feel better. Hungry, Goliath?' He purred like a kitten, so she went back in and got him a ham sandwich, which, magic man that he was, he made vanish in no time. 'Get in, boy!'

Get in? *Oh Lord no.* Couldn't she just have told him to trot on back to the *hacienda* and wait for us to get there?

'You coming, Bastion?'

'Be there in an hour or so. Just have to collect my internal fortitude that's spilled out all over the sand here.'

'This is super disappointing.'

I realized that I was acting like a worldly imbecile—acting like my druggie buddy Rufus, the antithesis of what I wanted to be in life. Victimized kid turns bully by being an incessant victim. The world is full of us, but I wanted nothing to do with it anymore. 'I'm sorry.' I got up from where I sat and got back in the car. Goliath nudged my neck from the back seat. I thought maybe I should say something. 'You miss picking fruit, Goliath?' My voice shook like a leaf in a hurricane. I distinctly saw several tears leak out and roll across his nose. Feeling sorry for him, I patted his head and rubbed his ears. 'Okay, buddy. We'll help you out of this hole. With God's help, we'll get you out.'

28

Acabado

We pulled up to *Casa Brillante* as if to visit close relatives on a Saturday afternoon. We were greeted by stalker Henri Avelar, dreamer Regario Nostrali, stalker Millaya Johnson, and dreamer Kiki Willow. Henri walked towards us. 'Come no further,' he commanded. 'Here, Goliath!'

Goliath stayed at my side.

'Goliath, won't you come in for tea?' asked Millaya as she also came toward us. Regario and Kiki, looks of solemn disquiet painted across their attractive features, turned together and disappeared behind the front door of the mansion.

Henri held up his hand against us. 'You are not welcome here, Bastion St. James. Neither are you, Aaron Sunderland. And take Goliath with you. You should all leave now, or we will assist you in doing so, but perhaps not in a way which may be so pleasing to you.'

'That sounds like a threat to me,' replied Aaron as she strode forward and brushed Henri with her shoulder.

Millaya intervened. 'You bring violence to *Casa Brillante*?'

I felt Goliath tense beneath my hand that rested on his neck.

'*Regnum coelorum vim patitur, et violenti rapiunt illud*,' said Aaron as she disappeared into the rambling house.[1] I and Goliath followed her. Neither of the sorcerers tried to stop us. When we were inside the main front room of the palatial *hacienda*, we stood alone, as if in an abandoned building. 'Come on, Bastion. Goliath and I know our way around.' The cougar-man ran ahead and up a spiral flight of stairs to the second story landing which overlooked the front room and had apparently been designed for grand entrances of the hosts to soirées filled with their regal guests and other VIPs. No parties like that had occurred since CG & Co. had purchased the property, of course, the house used now for the promulgation of 'flying sorcery,' described in some detail

---

[1] 'The kingdom of heaven has suffered violence, and the violent take it by force.' (Latin)

144

in Costanada's series of redundant books which only prove to be exciting to people who either have never known, or have forgotten, the Gift discovered by the Magi.

Mama Tilo emerged from one of the upstairs rooms and faced us, a defiant gaze in her black eyes. She said not a word as she raised in both hands crystal daggers and pointed them at us, intending our instantaneous deaths. Goliath, though, ran up the stairs faster than a squirrel in heat and knocked her down, and then bit her arm. She wailed bloody murder and thrashed around on the landing. Pain, for most people, is not something to be embraced and counted as joy; another of the many things that set Christians apart from the rest of the world—other, than, of course, our de-evolving, idiotic, Bronze Age propensity to mindlessly adhere to the archaic and contradictory scribblings of bygone agricultural desert shepherd bullies.

Goliath stood there like a man, and would have *actually* stood there like a man if he hadn't done something weird with sorcery and gotten himself trapped in the limiting body of a feline—similar to how druids trapped themselves inside of rocks embedded deep inside tree trunks so they could experience 'true magic,' they called it, on the day when the tree finally died, was cut down, and the stone broken apart in order to free them into the air. I'd say this famous line is pretty appropriate: '*Proclaiming themselves to be wise, they became like fools.*'

That said, Goliath seemed repentant, so if we confess what we have gone awry from love, God trusts us and is righteous enough to forgive us and cleanse us from all unrighteousness. A little extra work would be necessary in Goliath's cleansing process, but I'm a self-deceiving ass-wipe myself, so who am I to talk?

Aaron turned and went back down the stairs to the front chamber. Goliath and I followed. We were met by the remainder of the coven minus Mama Tilo, who could still be heard weeping upstairs. So much for being a matriarch of witches. So there we stood, faced off against Delia Minchin, Celia Durante, Emilia Blodmonath, Cordon Grey (who was no longer a tree log, by the way), Henri Avelar, Regario Nostrali, Millaya Johnson, Kiki Willow, and the two most formidable of them all—the usually congenial anthropologist-turned-brujo Arlo Costanada and the normally sweet-natured La Mora. The so-called 'Eagle' didn't come to save them, and there certainly materialized no John

Matanza, even in spirit, to give credit to their spiritual deceit.

Costanada stepped forward, the mastermind of the whole dog-and-pony show that feeds so many people with false hopes not only of magical earthly lives but of eternal life, yet failing to reveal exactly how to accomplish this feat of perception and perfection. When Jesus gave us the Beatitudes, it was his intent to show us that we *can't* follow any of them. His point? He came to, with his shared Presence, instill his power in us so that our righteousness could be accomplished in *his* nature, not ours too diseased with pride to accomplish anything except continual death and destruction. I saw nothing to come even remotely near God's strength or power in Arlo Costanada, and now my misgivings about the man have fully proved themselves out, since he has, in more recent years, been internationally proven to have been a fraudulent salesman of the caliber that puts P.T. Barnum, and certainly lesser snake-oil purveyors, to utter shame.

Aaron always surprised me, and this time was no different. As she stood with her feet apart and her hands loose at her sides, she spoke. '*Los seguidores de Jesús no tienen miedo. La muerte es un alivio para nosotros. Cuando se nos da trabajo por Dios para llevar a cabo, lo hacemos porque no tenemos ningún miedo de la muerte. Esta hacienda no es tuyo, y vas a salir ahora.*'[1]

I closed my eyes beneath the power of her words, and when I opened them again, I sat in my shadowy room at the Regency. As my eyes focused, I could see a figure opposite me, and was relieved that it was Aaron. *Hi!*

Then my bright kitchen light flipped on, and a dapper gentleman in his late 30s appeared in the doorway.

'Anybody up for some chow? I stepped down to the *Panda Express* a few minutes ago for some beef stir fry. Man, is it great to be back on two legs! By the way, Bastion, that ear rub earlier was nothing short of heavenly.'

---

[1] "Followers of Jesus have no fear. Death is a relief for us. When we are given work by God to carry out, we do it because we don't have any fear of death. This hacienda is not yours, and you're going to leave now."

29

Hollywood

You meet her in the mail,

and five months later you move from Northwest Florida to
Southern California. Because Jennifer says she loves you. In
every letter. At least three times. In every paragraph. You
can't stand it. You watch every Punk Rock movie you can
find; every documentary you can rent or borrow. Over and
over. You're 25. You already feel really old. Life has passed
you by. You just know it. You've got to catch up. Got to have
some fun. Live on the edge.

You have no idea what Los Angeles has in store.

♪

In the dawning all the night is gone
that holds my dearest comforting
things that I remember,
have never seen nor felt before—

Spirits haunting, yet disguised
in earthen vessels—
things a child so loves to feel,
and know, and see.

The morning of your leaving finally comes. Your little
sister Patsy, your only friend as a child, drives from twenty
miles away with glazed donuts. Your favorite. It's a special
memory you both share. You hug her tighter than you did
that day so long ago, on her sixteenth birthday. She begins to
cry. She kisses you. You call her sweetheart, and say you love
her. She breaks down.
The drive to the Pensacola bus station is quiet—filled with
childhood memories— and your mother's silent prayers.
Your last night at home is already gone, holding your dearest
comforts—things you will always remember. Things you feel
you *must* remember, but you're not sure why. You don't
understand. *Yet.* You don't know to love the treasure of each

moment. But you will. You will be blessed with life long enough to get there. But you don't know that either.

Your mother and dad see you to the bus door, tears in their tired eyes. They have together lived through the Great Depression and three terrible wars, but somehow you know this is the heaviest cross they have ever borne. They haven't slept all night, but they don't say that. You just know. Your mother tells the bus driver to please take care of her baby. He asks how old you are. She tells him, and he smiles and assures her that you'll be okay. Your dad holds you as tight as he ever has, then kisses your cheek. *I love you, son*, he says. For the first time in your life, you know he does. You fall apart. The driver hops off for a second. A boy about your age gets on, walks up to you and hands you a five dollar bill. 'Jesus told me to give you this,' he says, a nervous look in his dark, sad eyes. With no other words, he turns and exits. You sit stunned until the bus pulls away. You wave goodbye. You watch your mother collapse into your daddy's arms.

You show Jennifer's picture to every passenger who sits next to you. Even the flu-infested blonde fat guy that's asleep and crowding you out with his rump. He's mad at you for sitting with him. After all, he's sick, he says. You're scared you'll catch his fever. You show him the picture anyway. He acts nicer after that. The athletic blonde girl sitting across from you all the way from Mobile, Alabama to Phoenix finally calls you a Skinhead in El Paso, and says she hates Skinheads. You still think she's foxy. You've liked tomboys since you were three. She won't let anybody sit with her, even when the bus gets overcrowded. A loudmouthed AWOL Marine is eventually thrown off the Greyhound outside of Tucson by the cowboy bus driver who, as you remember, carried a sidearm. In the middle of the night at Needles, CA you are questioned about your American citizenship, because you look foreign and scared. You are scared, but your Southern accent embarrasses the Black border patrol officer. You are sorry he is humiliated. You hate the white-against-black stigma your drawl carries like indelible ink. In that very moment you vow to begin working on a more universal dialect. It takes you over a decade to perfect it, but you are happy with the results. You now sound like an Angeleno with a Southern twang. And your mannerisms are definitely L.A. Even people you meet who are from Los Angeles say 'Hollywood, right? Am I right?'

The Teachings of Don Luan

You have never experienced any state of consciousness even remotely resembling Hollywood, California. Truth is, you have always hated the idea of ever living 'Out There.' But now here you are. You call your Punk Rock girlfriend on the phone. She meets you. It's over before it starts. You rip up her picture. You get a job as a t-shirt salesman on Melrose Avenue and a room with a Muslim homicidal maniac on Hayworth in West Hollywood. A few months later, now living on Orange Drive just behind the Chinese Theatre, you land a good job at a bookstore in the Beverly Center—when it was still the place where all the stars shopped. Several women you meet there really like you; invite you to lunch, to their homes, into their beds. You tell each one she is beautiful, but you turn her down with a smile and a hug. 'You're my favorite girl,' you say, and mean every word. You're not a real Punk, you think sometimes. You're just angry at losing your childhood; at not really ever having one to speak of. But you don't come to this conclusion for another decade, and it's another decade before you realize that God had your back all along.

♪

You've lived in Hollywood a while now. But one August day, during the heat wave of '90, you are introduced to one of the deadliest sections of the city: the section of Santa Monica west from Vine. It doesn't look any deadlier than other sections of town. But as you approach it, you can feel something different. You shudder. There are worse places than this, you think. Your mind shoots to the day you got lost in Inglewood; to the night you got turned around in Venice, and lost. Both times on foot. Not funny.

You're on Vine heading north. It is noon. As you walk nearer to Santa Monica Blvd., your feelings scream out a warning. There's evil there like you've never felt before. Whatever it is seems to be stalking you. But you have to get to where you're going. An old friend from Pensacola has sent a package to the main Hollywood post office, and you're not sure where it is. It's your day off from work. A walk beats sitting around twiddling the thumbs. Later you'll take a bus to see your friends at work. You have no life.

At the northeast corner of this intersection of Vine and Santa Monica sits an Army supply store where in the recent past you've mulled over buying everything from an AK-47 to an Earthquake Survival Kit. Across the street from there, on the northwest corner, sprawls a full-service gas station, complete with green outdoor carpet. That's the part you've never explored. You've looked over at it, but only glanced down Santa Monica to the west.

The southern corners of this cross-street are littered with nondescript buildings. So are the morbid city blocks leading north and up to the famous HOLLYWOOD sign. Which sometimes at Christmas says HOLYWOOD. In the Summer of '87, you remember it said OLLYWOOD because somebody with ultra-right-wing influence wanted to honor Oliver North.[1] Rock musicians pouring into the city have forever tried to make the sign say HELLYWEIRD. But there aren't enough letters.

You know the area pretty well. You walk it all the time. Before dark. South of this noxious intersection, stretching down Vine toward Melrose Avenue, sit hundreds of unremarkable structures and graffiti-besmeared excuses for schools, burrito joints, laundry mats, check-cashing outfits, apartment dwellings. You live only a couple of streets from Melrose, on Willoughby. Street gangs divide up and control your city once pleasant and full of lively, contented children. This, of course, is according to nostalgic old-timers you've met at work. They now live in quaint desert strip-mall villages like Claremont and Montclair, but still enjoy making the drive into Hollywood. You have no reason to doubt their word. Most of them are originally from L.A. *They* were the children they're talking about.

It wasn't left to Beaver after all. Gun shots every night. Blood on the sidewalk every morning. After a few months living there, though, you get used to it. But one morning, nearly two years in, you awake and are suddenly terrified of your own nonchalance. An internal alarm forces you to reconsider. EVERYTHING. You don't even know why you're in L.A. to begin with. What was that girl's name? The one you bussed cross-continent from Florida to be with? It's been two interminable years. Was it Erica? Anika? No. Oh that's right. *Jennifer*. Jennifer Peacechild, she had called herself, fond of the Paisley Underground music movement.

---

[1] An American right-wing convicted criminal whose life was dedicated to destroying the equally despicable system of Socialism/Communism.

The Teachings of Don Luan

You like writing, but you're not a screenwriter. You're not a director. And you're certainly not an actor or a comedian, though your writer friends go to war with you on that last point. They want to groom you for standup comedy. Say they see dollar signs. Truth is, right now you don't work in 'the Biz' in any capacity, if you ever will. It's not what you moved here for.

You have no real reason to be in Hollywood. Yet, there's something enticing about it all. The glitz. The glamour. Casual strolls down the 'Boulevard of Broken Dreams.' The high-life of Sunset Strip. The funkiness of Melrose Avenue. The weird arrogance of Rodeo Drive. Fusty Hollywood Blvd. God-awful Venice Beach. The celebrity-studded Beverly Center where you slave as a 'Bookseller to the Stars,' making minimum wage, at exactly 39 hours a week, and not a second more. The 6-figure moguls in Connecticut are terrified of having to pay overtime.

You really can't afford to live in the nicer parts of town. You survive on ramen noodles and peanut butter as it is. Your coworkers all room with one another in the Fairfax District. Or West Hollywood. Even as far away as Westwood and the nicer sections of Venice. They beg you to move again. Move in with them if need be. Just get out of those parts of town. But you like it. You live in the same neighborhood Marilyn Monroe was a little girl in. Her orphanage, still running in fact, is right down the street from your apartment. And you've just moved from Humphrey Bogart's old flat, the one behind the Chinese Theatre. You lived there six months, drinking Shirley Temples at the *Carousel*, most likely with Charles Bukowski though you didn't recognize him, and studying Raymond Chandler like he was a god. Now you stay at home and drink bottled water, but the effect is still the same. You write the underbelly, and you can't get enough of it. Face it. You dream of being a Hollywood hack. Your nightmares are filled with film scores, loony tunes, and dead B-flick actors telling you who killed Roger Rabbit.

FEAR saturates your dreaded intersection of Santa Monica and Vine, which is not far from your actually very nice, and strikingly inexpensive, apartment. It's owned by the demure middle-aged Gay couple who live in front of you, sharing the happy little Oriental garden with you and your three other neighbors. George is a successful screenwriter; Jessie is a working actor. They both choose not to perceive the violence in the neighborhood that their 1930s rose-stucco chalet is built in. Gangs? What are those? You, on the other hand, live there for just that experience. You think. But you're not sure. You're tired of witnessing hoodlums in decrepit wing-tailed cars run over pet dogs. You're sick of LAPD choppers hovering overhead all night. You could use a little sleep. You're weary of hearing the gangster's mother scream—of watching her stand in apoplexy as her brother rushes Julio or Sergio or Chico to the ER. You realize you're out of place; in the wrong world. A world of hatred. *Is this really what I want to write about?* you ask yourself. You can't answer. The dead, fly-covered prostitute you saw on the corner of Willoughby and Vine that morning is still pretty fresh in your mind. Later you see her walking around again. A zombie. Apropos for Ed Wood's city, you muse. You wonder who would be interested in her services. Nicholas Cage whips his Saab into the 7-11 on the corner. You wonder what he's doing in this part of town. Studying a character, no doubt. Years later his massive body of tough-guy B-flicks supports your original thesis.

Ill intention slinks around Santa Monica and Vine at every angle, yet remains just outside of visual reach. This haunting atmosphere, you think, can only be described as fully lost. And therefore fully vengeful. Unforgiving. Your neighbor John Massari, film score writer, explains to you in detail how, just the year before, he witnessed a gang member kick a rival to death in the 7-11 while other gang members stood by the door so no one could come in, or out, until the murder had been completed.

Up and down Vine, spray-painted signs cover every wall and building. You choke in the thick exhaust fumes hanging in the air. You look out over the city to watch it suffocate beneath a deadly ochre cloud. A man walks by you. He has a gas mask on. A few minutes later another man comes along. He wears a sky blue t-shirt with a matching pair of baby underwear on his head. You double-take him, and he laughs like a maniac as he moves down toward Melrose. But he's still not as strange as the disturbed octogenarian starlets who sashay up and down Hollywood Boulevard, wearing evening gowns, strings of yellowed pearls, and faded feather boas.

As you head north on Vine, you begin to read the graffiti aloud, not caring if any of the few people out and about hear you. You figure you'll blend in with the other sane residents of Hollywood.

You read on the side of a hardware store,

The Teachings of Don Luan

DESOLATION

A credit union,
MINORITY
SEPARATION

On an elementary school,
GANG
DOMINATION

A check-cashing outfit,
HAVE YOU SEEN ME?

You realize the artist is a friend you still haven't met. You
smile. You near Santa Monica Boulevard. You notice again
the anger-driven dreadlocked Rastafarian who always works
at the service station, armed with his industrial-sized
janitors' broom, sweeping this gate of Hell. You correct
yourself. It's really more of a turnstile. He's there every day,
every day— all day. He stands guard, a permanent fixture at
the gas station; a lone sentinel.

You've never actually had to walk by him before. It's always
been the mercenary store and then back home, east side of
Vine up and back. You approach the intersection from the
south, planning to move through it and then west on Santa
Monica toward relatively calmer surroundings, and hopefully
a post office.

As you pass the Jamaican sentry, you surprise yourself.
You speak to him. Halting the conversation he is having with
a ball of filthy trash, he jerks around, growls and scuffs his
broom at you a few times. His jabbing yellow eyes are those
of a warrior. To your horror, though, you see that they no
longer house a soul. You scurry through his post like a
terrified alley cat.

A week later you leave Hollywood. You've enjoyed all you
can stand.

When the sun arises,
your Name is on my lips—I've seen
a thousand empty sunsets,
yet night is light about me.

August 1989

about the author

Bastion St. James, originally from Ferry Pass in Northeast Pensacola, Florida, relocated to Hollywood in the late 1980s while still in his 20s. He left that famous city 280 days later, but returned near the end of the decade and remained until the last few months of 1990, when he relocated to Venice. A writer by trade and passion, Bastion has made his home near Venice Beach with his creative wife Aaron since 1991. His mentor Donald Luan passed into eternity in 2013.

Ember Press

publishers of fine nonfiction